A. G. E Newland, J. D MacNabb

The Image of War

Service on the Chin Hills

A. G. E Newland, J. D MacNabb

The Image of War
Service on the Chin Hills

ISBN/EAN: 9783337167875

Printed in Europe, USA, Canada, Australia, Japan

Cover: Foto ©ninafisch / pixelio.de

More available books at **www.hansebooks.com**

THE IMAGE OF WAR,

OR

SERVICE ON THE CHIN HILLS.

BY

SURGEON-CAPTAIN A. G. E. NEWLAND,

I.M.S., 2nd Burma Battalion.

With an INTRODUCTORY HISTORICAL NOTE by

J. D. MACNABB, Esq., Political Officer, S. Chin Hills.

ILLUSTRATED WITH 191 PHOTOGRAPHS BY THE AUTHOR.

CALCUTTA:
THACKER, SPINK AND CO.
1894.

LIST OF FULL PAGE ILLUSTRATIONS.

8th Bengal Mountain Battery on the March	... *Frontispiece.*	
Mountain Stream in Chinland.		
Government Steamer landing Troops at Kalewa	*To face page*	1
Minywa, on Chin Frontier, starting point of the Boungshay Expedition	,, ,,	2
Officers of the Tashon Expedition	,, ,,	4
Camp at Minywn and Myettha River	,, ,,	6
Expedition marching into the Hills	,, ,,	9
Column crossing the Boinu River	,, ,,	10
Gurkha Coolie Camp : Mounting the Sanitary Guard ...	,, ,,	12
After the Day's Work	,, ,,	14
Waiting for inspiration ! Writing up the day's diary	,, ,,	16
Camp Toilet : getting ready for Dinner	,, ,,	18
Arrival of the Mail Bag in Camp	,, ,,	20
The 4th Madras Pioneers at work	,, ,,	22
In Camp : the Provost Marshal at Work ...	,, ,,	24
The Coolies' Camp Fire	,, ,,	26
A Halt : Gurhwallis and Coolies	,, ,,	30
How to climb a mountain	,, ,,	32
Getting Dhoolie up a stiff bit of mountain	,, ,,	34
Political Officer interviewing Chins	,, ,,	36
Descending a bad bit of mountain path : the Dawn Mountain	,, ,,	38
Head Quarters Camp at Munlipi (Klung-Klung)	,, ,,	44
Meeting of the two Columns at Tao ; sending off the news by Heliograph	,, ,,	46
We visit a Chin Chief : our reception	,, ,,	48
No. 2 Stockade at Foot of Chin Hills	,, ,,	50
The Wuntoo Chief's House (Klung-Klung). The largest and best house in the whole of the Chin Hills	,, ,,	54
The Political Officer obtaining information	,, ,,	56
Political Officer arranging about Coolies	,, ,,	58
Lao Var : a military post in the Klung-Klung Country ...	,, ,,	60
Falam	,, ,,	62
The occupation of Falam : the Column entering the Capital ...	,, ,,	63
Officers' quarters, Haka	,, ,,	70
Examining captured Arms	,, ,,	74
Officers bargaining with Chins	,, ,,	76
Fort White	,, ,,	80
The C. O. and his Staff-Officer interviewing a Chin Chief, "Old Tetapata"	,, ,,	82
A consultation : Mr. Carey, Mr. Macnabb, Major Howlett, and Capt. Evatt	,, ,,	86
Meeting of the Chiefs : the C. O.'s and the Political Officers of the Tashon and Nwengal Columns arranging their plan of compaign	,, ,,	88

154 SMALLER ILLUSTRATIONS INSERTED IN THE TEXT.

MOUNTAIN STREAM IN CHINLAND.
Thacker, Spink & Co., Calcutta.

GOVERNMENT STEAMERS LANDING TROOPS AT KALEWA, ON THE FRONTIER, FOR THE CHIN EXPEDITIONS.
Thacker, Spink & Co, Calcutta.

NOTE ON THE HISTORY OF THE CHIN HILLS,

BY

J. D. MACNABB, Esq., B.S.C., POLITICAL OFFICER, CHIN HILLS.

The great mountain ranges of Thibet and Central Asia send down, west and south of the supposed sources of the mighty Brahmaputra, a great offshoot or spur which, bounded by the valley of Assam and the plains of Bengal on the north-west, and, farther south, by the Bay of Bengal on the west, and by the valleys of the Chindwin and the Irrawaddy on the east, stretches in ever-narrowing ranges to the south, until as Cape Negrais, its last peak, it looks out on the Indian Ocean.

OFFICERS OF THE KLUNG KLUNG EXPEDITION.

These mountains are inhabited by various tribes, which, known under many different names, are alike at least in their barbarous instincts and raiding proclivities. In Bengal since 1844, and in Chittagong and Lower Burma since 1847, they have been a constant source of trouble and anxiety.

The history of our dealings with these tribes is one long tale of forbearance on our part, and unprovoked aggression on theirs, marked at but too frequent intervals by the murder of our most devoted frontier officers and the subsequent punitive expeditions. The conversion of Upper Burma into a British province changed our relations with these tribes, which thus had become surrounded by British territory, and could therefore no longer be treated as mere frontier tribes, with whom the less we had to do the better. The tribes in these hills bordering on Burma are usually known as Chins, and those bordering on Bengal and Assam as Lushais. The frequent raids committed on the plain villages by

LUSHAI FRONTIER POLICE.

these tribes called loudly for decisive action; and in 1888 matters were brought to a climax by the murder of Lieut. Stewart by the Lushais whilst surveying.

A punitive column was sent out to avenge this outrage in the open season of 1888-89, and the same year a force from Burma, under command of General Faunce, C.B., with Major Raikes, C.I.E., as Political Officer, was sent into the country of the Siyin tribe, who, refusing to submit or surrender their Burmese captives, had all their villages destroyed, and the post of Fort White was established.

INTRODUCTION. 3

In the open season of 1889-90 another expedition was organised, which was placed under command of Brigadier-General Symons, C.B., who was also given chief political powers, with Mr. Ross, Assistant Commissioner, and Mr. Carey, Assistant Commissioner, to assist him. This expedition, marching up from Pakoko to Kan, entered the hills much further south than the expedition of the preceding season, and, with but little resistance, occupied and established a post at Haka, the chief village of the Haka tribe, and visited Falam and the country round Haka. Another expedition from the Bengal side, under the command of General Tregear, C.B., advanced from Lungleh, and both parties making a mule track, they met at Haka, and thus established through communication between Burma and India. Both these expeditions found the malaria a worse enemy than the Chins and Lushais, and the troops suffered severely from fever.

OFFICERS OF THE BOUNGSHAY EXPEDITION.

During the open season of 1890-91, no arrangements were made for any expeditions on a large scale, but the murder of the Assistant Political Officer, Mr. Wetherell, by the Thettas necessitated the punishment of this village; and the first party not proving strong enough, a column of 250 rifles and two mountain guns, under Colonel Mainwaring, was sent up, *viâ* Gungaw, to Thetta, meeting another party from Haka. These two parties, combining, made an expedition into the Boungshay country to the south, going as far as Shurkwa. Although the Boungshay Chins had made great preparations for resistance and built numerous stockades, they lost heart at the last and offered but little resistance to the troops.

INTRODUCTION.

The season closed by a rising of the Klung Klung tribe, who attacked a party of troops accompanying the Political Officer on a peaceful errand to meet the Political Officer of South Lushai at Tao, in April, but the Manipur disaster tied our hands and prevented immediate punishment being inflicted on this tribe. In the northern Chin Hills much had been done to bring the Kanhows under control, and a new post had been established at Tiddim.

This season did not effect much improvement in our position in the hills, except to make it evident that it was not sufficient to occupy isolated posts in

OFFICERS OF THE BURMA AND BENGAL COLUMNS AT TAO VILLAGE.

the hills to stop the raiding in the plains, but that it was incumbent on us to bring all the Chin tribes under control.

To effect this in the open season of 1891-92 the following columns were organized :—

FIRST—The Boungshay Column, commanded by Major Gunning, K.R.R., and consisting of 250 rifles and two mountain guns, was directed to explore and bring under our control the Boungshay tribes south of Haka.

OFFICERS OF THE TUSAYAN EXPEDITION

INTRODUCTION. 5

SECOND—The Klung Klung Column, of the same strength, and commanded by Major Browne, D.S.O., 39th Gharwal Rifles, was directed to punish the Klung Klung tribe for their attack on our troops in April, 1890.

THIRD—The Tashon and the Nwengal Columns, consisting of 300 rifles and two mountain guns each, and commanded respectively by Major Howlett, 2nd Burma Battalion, and Captain Hugh Rose, were directed to occupy and establish a post at Falam and bring the Tashon tribe and their tributaries under our control.

FOURTH—The Kanhow Column, under command of Captain Stevens, 4th M.P., and consisting of 250 rifles and two mountain guns, was directed to visit the Kanhows and tribes north of them, and to open up communication with Manipur.

OFFICERS AND SERJEANTS OF THE KING'S ROYAL RIFLES WHO TOOK PART IN THE EXPEDITIONS.

All these columns were successful, and accomplished their work without fighting. Towards the end of the season, however, small outbreaks occurred at Shurkwa and Botoung, both of which were suppressed without trouble, the Chins suffering heavy loss at Shurkwa. Troubles had, however, been gathering in Lushailand, and the end of the season saw a general rising both in North and South Lushai, which was suppressed with some difficulty, as strong reinforcements had to be sent to Forts Aijal and Lungleh, and a column had to march across from Fort White to relieve the Superintendent of South Lushai in the face of great difficulties, upon which the rising collapsed.

INTRODUCTION.

Such is an outline of the history of the Chin-Lushai Hills. It is a land that produces nothing but the savages who inhabit it. A thorn in the sides of all who have to do with it, it has no future, and appears capable of no development. I have never met an officer who has been in them whose dearest wish it has not been to get out of them!

TOUNGTHAS WOMEN ON THE CHIN FRONTIER.

For troops it is a most trying country to campaign in. Approached through malarious valleys and *terai* which decimate the troops with sickness before they reach the inhabited heights,

OLD FALAM : WHERE PERMANENT POST WAS BUILT.

they are then rewarded by constant marching over a succession of razor-backed

INTRODUCTION.

mountains and over paths so bad that sometimes it is only with infinite difficulty that five miles a day are accomplished.

Except it be to rush a stockade, seen, and fighting consists of marching along a precipitous path in Indian file and being picked off by an invisible enemy. What may be the immediate future of the Chin Hills it is impossible to foretell, but it is to be hoped that the Chins will in due time settle down into peaceful and law-abiding subjects of Her Majesty the Queen-Empress.

TROOPS MARCHING UP THE FRONTIER.

J. D. M.

HAKA, CHIN HILLS, *June, 1892*.

THE IMAGE OF WAR;
OR,
SERVICE ON THE CHIN HILLS.

A CAMP IN THE HILLS—KLUNG-KLUNG COUNTRY.

E WILL not weary the reader by detailed descriptions of the expeditions. To give a minute account of the various expeditions into these hills would not only be foreign to our purpose, but would be monotonous and uninteresting. Our object is not to weary the reader, but rather to entertain him by the few rambling notes we shall jot down, which will, we hope, help him to understand the pictures and to gather an idea of what service on these hills is like.

Our Experiences are Common.

Mr. Macnabb has told us briefly of the various expeditions into these hills, and the work they have accomplished. The streams we waded through, the hills we climbed, the *khuds* we slipped down, the food we ate, the sickness that laid us low, the odorous Chins we met everywhere, the freezing cold, the drenching rain; afterwards the sweltering heat in the deep jungle-clothed valleys; all these varied scenes of camp-

TROOPS CROSSING A RIVER ON THE FRONTIER.

SHELLING A HOSTILE VILLAGE—"LOADING."

life, though wanting in the excitements of actual warfare but with all its discomforts, were the common experiences of all the expeditions. The experience of one is, therefore, the experience of all. "But," in the slightly altered words of a well-known writer, "let it not be imagined for a moment that these inhospitable hills or the hard life had in the least suppressed the spirit of making the best of things, which is common to the Anglo-Saxon blood wherever found."

COLUMN CROSSING THE HOJNU RIVER.
Thacker, Spink & Co. Calcutta.

Our Transport.

Owing to the mountainous nature of the country, the transport of the columns consisted mainly of Indian hill coolies, supplemented, as occasion required, by Chins. The Chin, when he can be obtained, is an excellent beast of burden. He is quite at home in these hills, and thinks nothing of running up the steepest with eighty pounds or more slung on his back. They also carry their own food, thus giving the commissariat no trouble on that score.

SHELLING A HOSTILE VILLAGE—"FIRE!"

In some of the expeditions, where mule-tracks had been previously made, mule transport to a limited extent was employed in addition to the coolies. These coolie corps were enlisted in Darjeeling, and brought across specially for these operations. Each corps was in charge of a British officer. A surgeon was also attached to each.

SHELLING A HOSTILE VILLAGE—"JAMMED."

A Chat about the Coolies.

These Gurkha and Bhœtia coolies were a cheery lot of little fellows. At first, coming through the *terai*, many were knocked over by illness, and about a hundred were more or less *hors de combat.* But those who kept their health worked very well indeed, and, once we were well in the hills, the sickness among them greatly diminished. They were nailers at ferreting out fowls or pigs in deserted villages. They always discovered the yam and sweet potato fields sooner than anyone else, with the exception of the Chin friendlies, whom they ran very close. On the march, too, they were always discovering edible roots of all kinds, which they dug up and munched as they went along. On arrival in camp, they deposited their loads, and then

CHIN COOLIES: RESTING AND FEEDING ON THE MARCH.

there was a rush to the site told off for them to secure the best spots. Then they raced off to the jungle, and with their handy *kukries* they cut down trees and branches, and in a very short time they had built themselves "lean-tos" and had commenced their culinary operations. They always appeared to be in the best of spirits. They seemed to look down upon the Chin, and thought he had no right in the country at all. When they first came into these hills, they were provided by Government with a complete outfit, from boots to great-coats. On the first few marches you saw them lost in a heap of clothing and struggling along in loose ill-fitting boots. But gradually the things disappeared one by one. The boots were the first to go; and by the end of the operations they did not turn out in a superabundance of clothing.

GURKHA COOLIES: HOW THEY CARRY THEIR LOADS.

GURKHA COOLIE CAMP: MOUNTING THE SANITARY GUARD.
Thacker, Spink & Co., Calcutta.

In camp they were very handy too. They brought in fire-wood or built us shelters or helped in constructing defences. Many of the Bhoetias attached themselves as cooks to the soldiers' messes on the chance of picking up scraps. They helped in slaughtering mythun and goats also on the chance of getting the remains. It was a curious sight to watch the long line of pigmies tramping up a hill with their loads. From time to time they halted in groups, resting their loads on sticks, or on convenient banks or rocks, to ease their backs; and every time they did this, each man emitted a long shrill whistle of relief, by which you could tell in the densest forest when the coolies were in the neighbourhood.

GURKHA COOLIE CAMP: TELLING OFF COOLIES FOR DAY'S WORK.

At first there was considerable difficulty in finding your coolie or your kit in camp. But subsequently, when they got to know the various *sahibs* and their regiments, and fell into the daily routine, there was no more trouble in this respect. Sometimes, however, your coolie went sick on the march, and, perhaps, a relief had to be sent back from camp. This would delay your kit, and on one or two occasions some of us were kept without our bedding in this way till nearly midnight.

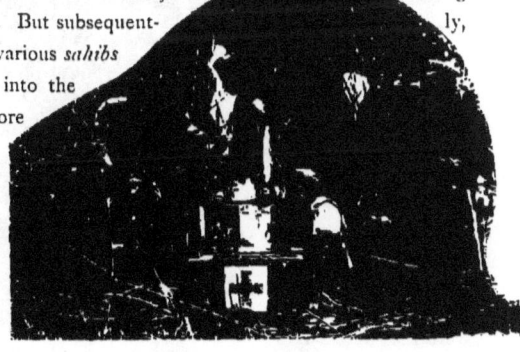

GURKHA COOLIE CAMP: MEDICINE TIME.

There were always a number of spare coolies with

the rear-guard to bring on the loads of men, who, from sickness or other causes, were unable to do so themselves. However, we had nothing to complain of on this head as, after the first few marches, our kits were usually first into camp.

They had a certain amount of *esprit de corps*, too, in a small way, and when a comrade went sick on the march and could not get along, though they did not appeal to his patriotic feelings to induce him to make one final effort to reach camp—like the soldier who, to encourage his sick and weary comrade who had lain down on the road-side and refused to march any farther, entreated him to "make a heffort, Bill! Old England knows what you're a-doin' of!"—yet they did their best to help the man along, often carrying him and his load too, in addition to their own, when no spare coolies were available, so that there might be no complaints against their corps.

COOLIES CARRYING BAGGAGE OF COLUMN ACROSS A RIVER.

Our Servants make us Swear!

Our servants, as a rule, gave us the most trouble. Although they had no-thing but themselves to carry up the hills, yet they usually managed to arrive in camp the last of all! And till they came, there was no getting a cup of hot tea or having your man- sion erected. It often made us use violent language, but who could blame us?

A chat about our tents and things.

No tents were taken with any of the columns, except for the hospital; nor were they necessary. After a little experi- ence the men soon learned to run up very snug shelters of leaves covered with their waterproof sheets. Immediately on

ON THE MARCH: COOLIES RESTING.

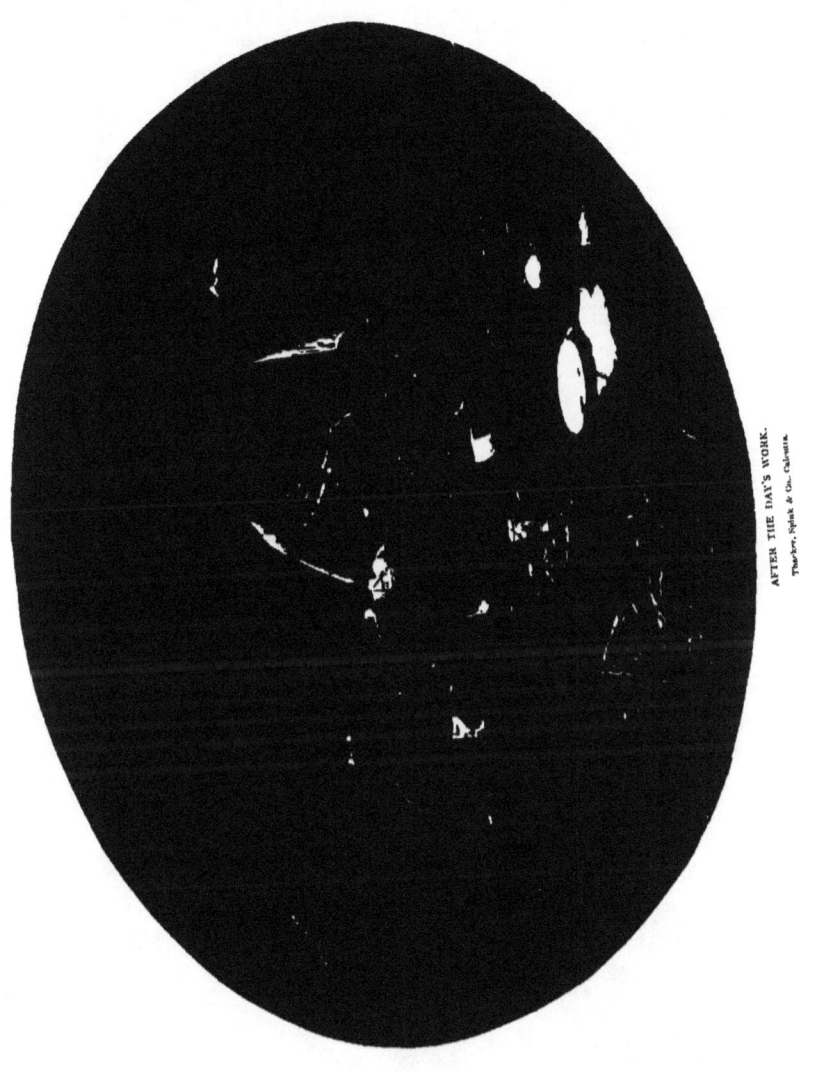

AFTER THE DAY'S WORK.
Thacker, Spink & Co., Calcutta.

arrival in camp the men set to work, and within an hour everyone was comfortably settled down in his own shelter.

In work of this kind, and in clearing the jungle, &c., the men armed with *kukries* had a great pull over their comrades in arms who were not so armed. Many of the men invested in these knives, buying them at high prices from the Gurkha coolies. Every officer too had provided himself with one. It would be an excellent thing if, on service of this description, all troops, British and Native, were furnished with *kukries*.

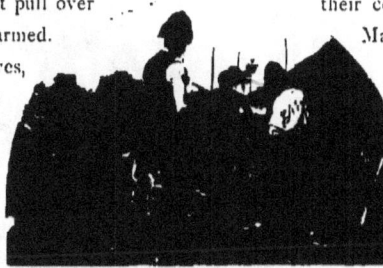
OFFICERS GIVING A HELPING HAND.

Most of the officers had brought out miniature tents of many varieties. They were just high enough to crawl under, and they kept off the dew at night. They were very light, and came within the total of 40 lbs. of baggage allowed to each officer. Those who had no tents stretched their waterproof sheets over a pole and slept under them— and a waterproof sheet of decent size makes a very excellent tent. It keeps off the dew and rain, and that is all that is necessary in work of this kind.

ARRIVAL OF COOLIES IN CAMP WITH RATIONS.

Our tents sometimes give trouble.

Sometimes, however, a strong breeze would spring up at night and our miniature tents, if not securely pegged down, would topple over, and the muffled volley of language that escaped from below the folds of cloth was "quite frightful to hear," as Truthful James would have remarked. Then crawling out into the cold, dark, shivery night, the irate ones would have to re-erect their fallen tents as best they might. For, as usually happens, to lay your hands on your match-box when you wanted it, would be about the last thing to occur; and, when you did find it, to strike a light in a gale of wind would be impossible; and to find your servant in the dark would be equally hopeless—though you wished much to give him a rude awakening for his carelessness in not securing your tent firmly. If you attempted to go in search of him you would either upset someone's tent or shelter, or fall over the *khud* yourself, which would be far worse; and you cannot shout lest you rouse and alarm the whole camp; and so, fumbling in the dark and with much vexation of spirit, you at last succeed in re-erecting your abode, into which you once again crawl and turn into your blankets; or, perchance, if your patience and temper are not up to the strain, you drag your blankets out of your tent and lie *on* your tent, vowing vengeance on your scoundrelly boy!

GARHWALLIS BUILDING SHELTERS.

GURKHA COOLIES BUILDING SHELTERS.

We dilate on the Weather.

During the months of November, December, and January the cold is intense on these hills, the temperature falling below freezing-point at night. The water

WAITING FOR INSPIRATION! WRITING UP THE DAY'S DIARY.
Thacker, Spink & Co., Calcutta

freezes in our basins, and the ground in the morning is found covered with hoar frost. Marching can be done the whole day. A strong wind usually prevails, and this makes the cold more keen and cutting. Breasting the stiff hills, one gets warmed up to a red heat; but, when you reach the acclivities, the cold wind goes through you like a knife and makes you shiver to your bones.

To keep oneself warm at night, there is nothing like having one's blankets sewn up into a bag.

In March and April rain falls, and in the low-lying valleys the heat is very considerable about this time, and marching after 8 or 9 o'clock a.m. a terrible grind. The regular rains set in about May or June, and no operations are then possible.

Our Camp Furniture.

Our baggage being on such a limited scale, such luxuries as chairs and tables did not encumber us. After the day's work is done, clad in our greatcoats, we sit on the ground round the roaring camp-fire smoking our pipes and chatting till dinner is announced.

Dinner-Time in Camp.

The grunts and shouts of satisfaction with which this announcement is received testifies that everyone is fortified with that greatest of all blessings—a keen appetite. The meal is a frugal one, consisting mainly of bulli-beef and the omnipresent *murghi*, done in various ways, chiefly stewed, boiled or curried—the limits of our *chef's répertoire*. Sometimes these are supplemented with a few odds-and-ends we may have been able to bring up with us. Eggs, too, we usually have in abundance. Your own or your servant's bedding, rolled up into a bundle and deposited between your legs, provides the table on which you dine; or if the commissariat can give you some empty deal cases, in which beef or biscuit tins are packed, they make excellent tables.

Our Servants again.

Our servants are a motley crew. There are representatives from the north, south, east and west of India, as well as from Burma, and even beyond. They apparently do not give their masters complete satisfaction, if one is to judge by the language one hears on all sides, not only

OUR SERVANTS.

at dinner time, but also the last thing at night and the first thing in the morning :—

"Are you not going to give me something to eat, you villain?"

"Why mayn't I have something to drink?"

"Blue blazes! the cook has made this curry too hot!" shouts someone, as he mops his perspiration-bedewed brow, and his eyes water and twinkle from the warmth of the curry.

"No! it's an excellent curry!" shout others in derision; "it's not a bit hot."

"What have you done with the cold fowl and eggs, you rogue?"

"Done giving to dogs, master!"

"You incarnation of a liar!"

"You'll all have your pay cut. De'il a sou will any of you get this month."

"You have drunk the rum, you scoundrel. I'll thrash you! Get out of my sight!"

"I speak true word, master; I no drink. Rum fall out on way."

CAMP TOILET: GETTING READY FOR DINNER.

Thacker, Spink & Co., Calcutta.

Interrogations and exclamations of this sort vary the monotony of the dinner hour. The fusilade, however, falls harmlessly on our *nowkers*, who go on pretty much as usual, and know that master soon forgets his terrible threats of vengeance, and that the heavy fines so freely inflicted are never cut at the end of the month.

One servant must have made his master very angry indeed one day, for we have a vivid recollection one freezing morning of seeing an apparition in pyjamas rush out of his tiny tent with bare feet, regardless of the cold, and, seizing with both hands the first thing he got hold of, which happened to be a large log, he belaboured his *nowker*, and then, panting and out of breath, he dived back into his tent to recover his second wind.

Post-prandial Enjoyments.

Dinner is washed down with rum or whisky, if there is any, or with a hot cup of tea or cocoa. Then, with our pipes and nightcaps of something comforting in our mugs, we sit or lie round the blazing fire talking over the events of the day or relating our mutual experiences, our *raconteurs* shining on such occasions. Some of the circle sometimes burst into melody; but this was, I confess, not often—we appeared to be an unmusical lot; or we often arranged the outline of the annual Chin dinner we decided to institute in London, in which roast pork and bulli-beef would largely figure, and the chief drink would be "*Yu*," the details being left for future consideration; and so, Alnaschar-like, we built many castles in the air, which the last post-bugle usually shattered, as it told us it was time for bed. Many were the stories, veracious and otherwise, that enlivened our camp-fires. We learnt how the Chin ladies helped in making gunpowder; how a gallant officer, mistaking the hooting of monkeys for the war-cry of the Chins, rapidly got his guns into action; and how, many years ago, an Englishman who had been captured from Burma, had been walked through Chin-land, with certain duties to perform. These and many others we heard, but they will not bear repeating here. Our post-prandial gathering round the camp-fire was always an enjoyable time. The wine, it is true, did not flow, because we had none, and the rum and whisky were limited; but we hoped for better things, and for the time were content : and we know that a contented mind is a continual feast—or at least they tell us so.

The Junior does Stoker.

To the junior officer present usually fell the duty of stoking the fire. Sometimes the one nearest the fire, as deriving the most benefit from it, was called upon to do this in this fashion : — " Sawbones, you are nearest the fire —very cold night—fire going out—lots of wood!" Then Sawbones reluctantly got up and stoked. This method of expressing oneself after a time became quite popular. One constantly heard orders like this :—"Boy! lots of whisky—lots of mugs—we are very dry!" " Boy ! lots of fowls —lots of eggs—we are very hungry — lots of stew—lots of omelettes!"

IN CAMP: A DOG FIGHT.

A Nightmare.

On one occasion we had been discussing the possiblity of a night-attack. This, with some heavy pastry our cook had inveigled us into eating, had so affected one young officer that, in the middle of the night, he gave us all a start by jumping out of his bed and with quivering frame and outstretched arms shouting out :— " The Chins are upon us ! Here they are at last !! Look out !!!" It was only a nightmare.

IN CAMP : OFFICERS PATCHING DAMAGED CLOTHING.

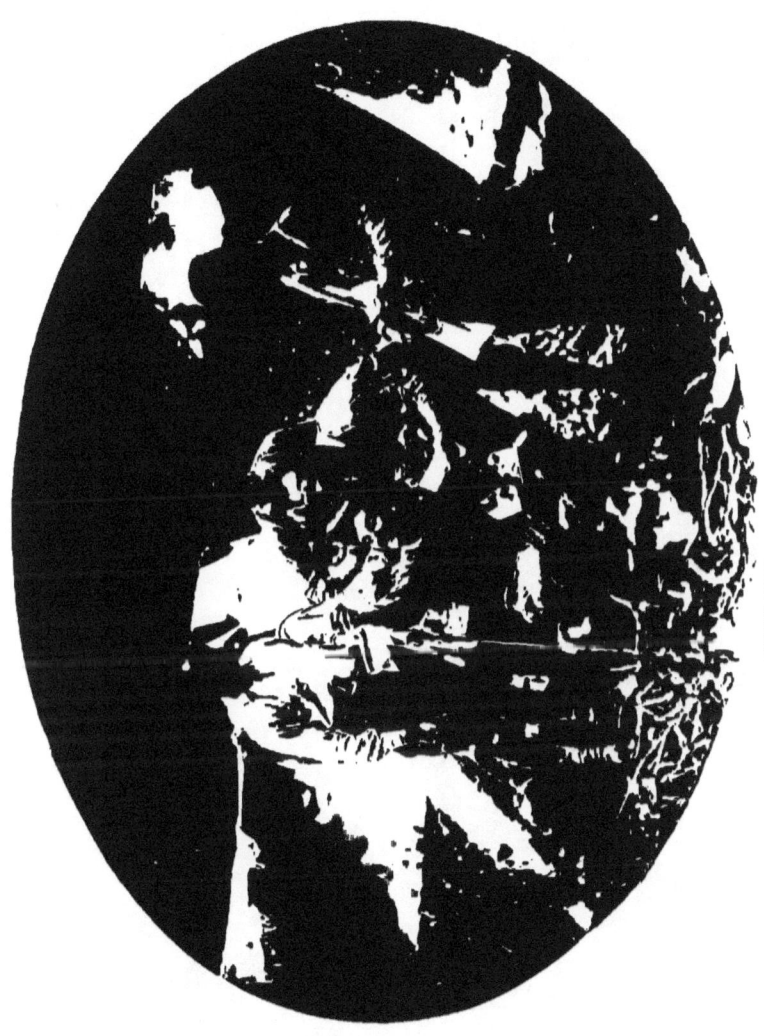

ARRIVAL OF THE MAIL BAG IN CAMP.
Thacher, Spink & Co., Calcutta.

How we had a night-scare.

We were not often troubled by night-alarms. A Chin hates going about in the dark, he is too afraid of his *Nats;* so they have never made attacks by night. On one occasion only was there a night scare; but we found over-indulgence in "*Yu*" or Chin beer was the cause of it all. The Political Officer, who, with an escort of sepoys and his friendlies, was sleeping in the Chief's house in a village near which the troops were camped, sent down to the camp at midnight to say that the people of the village and his friendlies were in a great state of excitement, expecting momentarily to be attacked by a neigbouring hostile village. It was a dark and bitterly cold night, but the hard-worked Staff Officer had to jump out of his blankets, rush up the hills, and warn all the guards and pickets to be on the alert. The night, however, passed away quietly enough and nothing happened; and it transpired in the morning, much to the disgust of our worthy Staff Officer, that the whole village had been having a big drink, and the scare had been evolved out of their *Yu*-besotted imaginations!

BREAKFAST BEFORE THE START.

SADDLING-UP FOR THE MARCH.

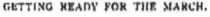
GETTING READY FOR THE MARCH.

Undressing for Bed.

It was very unpleasant tearing ourselves away from the genial glow of the fire. Most of us dreaded changing into our night things in our cold tents, so our servants brought the things to the fire and warmed them. When it was time for bed, we changed into them, and then made a rush for our tents and tumbled into our blankets, where we often shivered through the night, if our tents let in the cold blast—as they often did, if one had not taken the precaution of piling up leaves and grass all round them or throwing up a small embankment or earthwork, as one officer was very expert in doing.

THE 8TH BENGAL MOUNTAIN BATTERY HALTED ABOVE FALAM.

Shows how some People cannot Sleep.

A hard day's work, as a rule, produces a good night's sleep; but there are some funny people who cannot sleep after a certain hour in the morning. One such always shouted for his servant at an early hour, the moment he awoke. This call, regularly piercing

KING'S ROYAL RIFLES READY FOR THE MARCH.

THE 4TH MADRAS PIONEERS AT WORK.
Thacker, Spink & Co., Calcutta.

the morning air, was as good as the bugler's "rouse." Most of us found it so, and thought the bugle-call later on quite superfluous. Another sleepless warrior we had too. He usually awoke with the lark, or earlier, and in the intervals of shouting and swearing at his boy for being late with his early tea and "*chupatties*," he treated us to snatches of melody in various keys.

We have a Pestilence of Dogs.

A HALT: OFFICERS HAVING BREAKFAST.

Dogs we had with us in abundance. They usually got between our legs on the march; and when you reached your tent at night, you usually found a few of your friends' dogs snugly ensconced within your blankets. To swear at and *houk* them out was the work of a moment; but they were not to be put off in that way, for next night you would be sure to find them in your tent again, or perhaps they would grow bold, and, as soon as you fell asleep, they would again crawl in and lie on you; and all night long you would dream that somehow, like another Atlas, you were carrying the Chin Hills on some part of your body, though you could not tell which; and in the morning you would wake up to find that you had not been troubled with a nightmare, as you thought, from indulging too freely in those thick slices of frozen bulli-beef and rum, but that it was those infernal dogs of your friends. Sometimes they fought and barked at night, as is their wont, and caused general irritation, but it was too cold for anyone to rush after them with sticks. We could only throw boots or other handy missiles at them, but they kept well out of reach as a rule.

ON THE MARCH:
FIVE MINUTES HALT AT A STREAM TO DRINK.

The Dog Snores.

One officer had a huge dog, which shared his tent with him. At night loud sounds, like strong, healthy human snoring, always proceeded from that tent; but the occupant always would have it that it was the dog that made the noise. But "we had our doubts," as the Chin Chiefs remarked, when we told them that we had come into their country solely for their own good.

A nocturnal Mule gives trouble.

Sometimes a mule would break loose from his tethering at night and come strolling around, knocking up against our tents, or, perhaps, upsetting a few, and causing great excitement among our canine friends. And till that rampaging beast was captured and tethered again there was no peace for us; for you never knew when he might

FIVE MINUTES HALT AFTER A STIFF CLIMB.

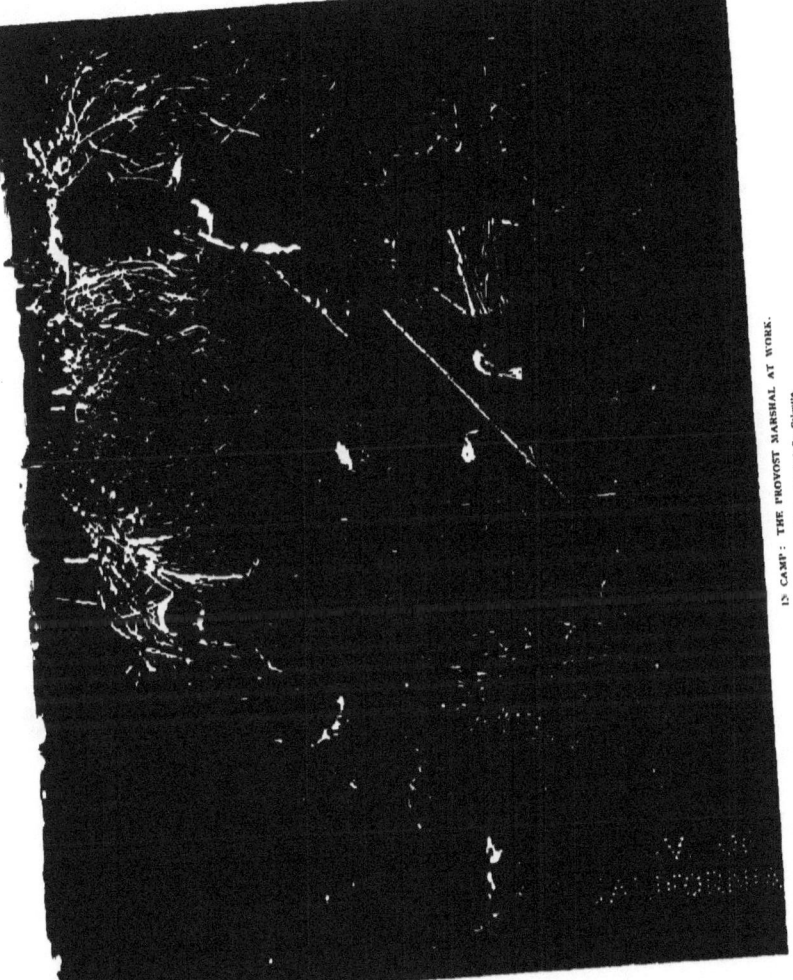

15 CAMP: THE PROVOST MARSHAL AT WORK.
Thacker, Spink & Co., Calcutta.

not come charging up against your tent and putting his gentle foot down on some tender part of your body.

Our Servants become noisy.

Servants are a most garrulous lot, especially the old ones. They would sit up around the fire, after their masters had retired, and suck and gurgle away at their *hubble-bubbles*, and talk and talk between whiles, till some irate *sahib*, who could stand it no longer, would shout and swear at them; and then, with a pious exclamation regarding the irritability of the *sahib*, they would roll themselves in their blankets and tumble off to sleep.

ADVANCE GUARD HALTED TO LET REST OF COLUMN CLOSE-UP BEFORE ENTERING VILLAGE.

The Dhoolie-bearer begins to cough.

When these, at last, became silent, the dhoolie-bearers would begin wheezing and coughing—and they beat anyone at this. They appeared always to wait till everything had become perfectly quiet, and then they began. If you heard a very bad whine, and a long drawn-out wheeze, it was pretty sure to come from a *kahar*. He seems to lay himself out for a good prolonged fit when he begins, and he helps on the process by sucking deeply of

A HALT: KING'S ROYAL RIFLES AND FRIENDLIES.

his *hubble-bubble*. It is a fine art with these people; a cough and a wheeze that rise in intensity gradually, and, when the climax of enjoyment is reached, the paroxysm ends with a long-drawn sigh of "*Ram! Ram!*"

So we always kept people of such peculiar habits a long way off, if possible. But often, on account of the limited space, we were all crowded together, and then the wheezy followers' enjoyment would be cut short at intervals by the stentorian "*chuprao!* you sir-r!" from the *sahibs*' neighbouring tents.

The Coolies are Musical.

The Gurkha coolies woke about one or two o'clock in the morning, and began cooking their food at that early hour. They could not sleep for the cold, and no doubt preferred sitting round the fire. Some would often break out into song, accompanied by a monotonous drubbing on a drum which they always carried about with them. But these early concerts were apparently not appreciated by the *sahibs*, for a shout would presently come from one tent for the "*budmashes* to *chuprao!*" The coolies would wait a minute or two, and resume their music when they thought the *sahibs* had gone off to sleep again. But again would come the "*chuprao!* you b——s!" from several tents,

THE BHISTI ON HIS ROUNDS.

KING'S ROYAL RIFLES COOKING THEIR DINNERS.

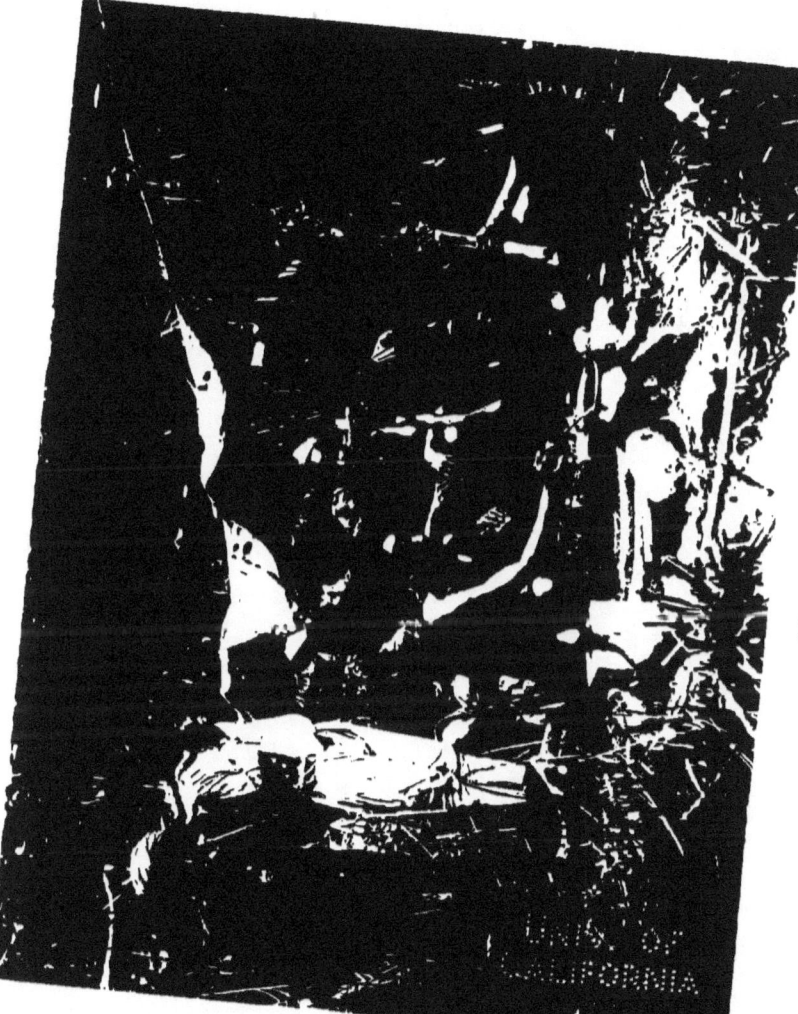

THE COOLIES' CAMP FIRE.
Thacker, Spink & Co., Calcutta.

and the poor musically-inclined coolies would have to desist, wondering why the *sahibs* should be so irritable and unappreciative of early morning song.

Our Servants get Tipsy.

Our servants, sometimes from too free indulgence in their masters' rum or whisky bottles, became tipsy; and though it was annoying enough to the man whose spirits had disappeared, it very often afforded us much amusement. One servant argued that he did not drink his master's rum, but some other *sahib's*, and he therefore thought his own master ought not to grumble in return for this considerate conduct of his !

SEPOYS COOKING.

Our servants were also particular in the company they kept. They had their own sets, and when one set succeeded in stealing or eating or drinking more than another set, there was a row, in which we were often called upon to interfere.

We Renounce Shaving.

Shaving on the march being too much of a grind, especially as you could never get hot water when you wanted it and your razor refused to keep sharp, it was not generally practised. Most of us, however, in our scrubby beards, looked terrible guys; some were positively awful! One energetic officer, however, was not to be denied his morning shave. There you saw him regularly sitting before his tent, with a rug wrapped round him, shivering in the freezing cold and scraping away at his chin with the greatest

IN CAMP: SEPOYS AND COOLIES BATHING.

enjoyment. It must have been a blunt razor too, for the grating it produced could be heard in all our tents.

We Clip our Hair.

Hair-brushing, too, was a superfluous luxury, so most of us had our heads clipped down to the skin with mule shears. It did not improve our appearance, but, on the contrary, we looked remarkably like a batch of released convicts. However, it was comfortable, though decidedly cold at night. One officer revelled in the delights of a nightcap, and he did not mind; but the rest of us, who had come unprepared for this contingency, had to sleep in our forage-caps. If clippers were not available, the company-barber (either European or native) performed on us with equal success.

IN CAMP: WAITING FOR SOMETHING TO EAT.

We abandon Tubbing—Shocking!

Our bathing arrangements were primitive, and generally done in our basin or pony-buckets. At first we tried bathing in the streams, but this was always followed by fever, and we had to give it up. With the intense cold and other drawbacks, no one rose to regular tubbing. It could not be done at any price; and "when you cannot do what you will, you must do what you can;" that is, we did without it, like our friends the Chins, except

IN CAMP: POLITICAL OFFICER HAVING FRIENDLY CHAT WITH HIS FRIENDLIES.

when we halted at a place for a day or two and were able to rig up a bathing-place.

Our Kit becomes ragged.

With our 40 lbs. of kit, it was not much in the way of clothing one could carry about. Hard wear and tear soon reduced our scanty kit to a ragged condition. It was not unusual, after the day's work was done and we lay about under the trees, to see someone engaged in patching his tattered garments in a manner that would have done credit to any tailoring establishment. When there was a halt, our servants had a general washing up, which usually reduced our ragged belongings to a further state of raggedness.

STAFF OFFICER PAYING CHIN COOLIES.

Our Boots.

With the hard marching, our boots soon came to grief—much sooner than we had bargained for. Many of us were reduced to investing in shoe-leather from followers who preferred climbing hills with unclothed feet. A collection of our boots, at the end of the operations, would have been a curious sight.

Our "tout ensemble."

And so, clothed in torn, toil-stained garments, with unkempt scrubby beards

IN CAMP: A QUIET CHAT BEFORE DINNER.

and convict-cropped heads, with your pedal extremities in shreds of boots, and your manly legs enveloped in frayed *putties*, even your most familiar friends would have failed to recognise you.

Our Marches.

Owing to the dark, damp, misty mornings the day's march rarely began before 7 or 8 o'clock. Everything was packed and ready for the start a quarter of an hour or so previously, and everyone had partaken of a substantial meal. Then the march began; but the progress was slow, owing to the many ranges of hills that had to be climbed and the bad paths. There were frequent halts to enable the Pioneers to make the paths practicable for the transport or the gun— mules. In many places a new path had to be zig-zagged all the way up a steep hill, or huge fallen trees had to be cleared away. All this entailed much hard and continuous work on everyone. Even to those who had nothing to do on such occasions, the long halts, cramped up as everyone was on narrow paths on steep mountain sides, were very wearying and fatiguing.

IN CAMP: DISCUSSING THE POLITICAL SITUATION.

The Mules fall down the "khuds."

In spite of every precaution many mules, especially the battery animals, fell over the *khuds*, and some were killed outright or were so badly damaged that they had to be shot. Many had wonderful escapes.

INTELLIGENCE OFFICERS AT WORK.

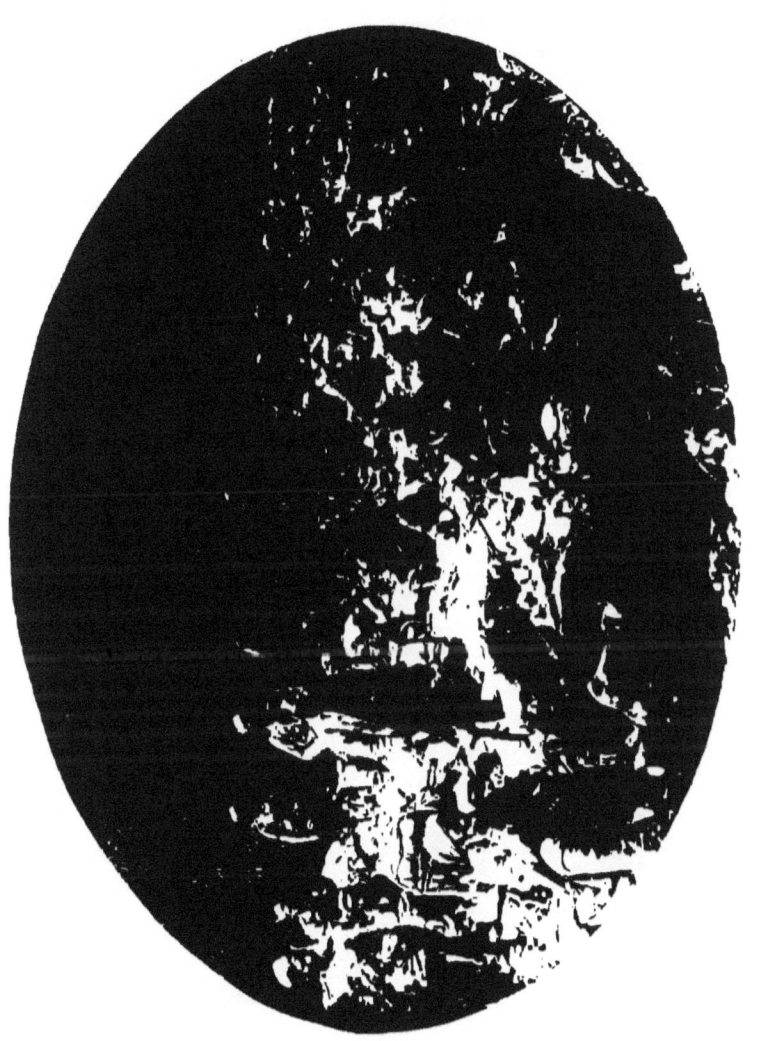

A HALT: GURHWALLIS AND COOLIES.
Thacker, Spink & Co., Calcutta

When we got into the bad hilly country, these accidents were constantly happening —that is, falling down the *khuds*. Some obstinate mules, like Old Father William, "did it again and again." But by constant practice some had become so expert, that they managed to pick themselves up in some very hairy places in a most astonishing manner, without sustaining the least damage. One animal we saw drop down 40 feet on to a mass of rocks. We thought he was killed; but presently he got up and shook himself, and, when he was brought up to the path again, he was found to have been hurt in no way.

Mule Stories.

Talking of mules, our artillery officer often told us curious stories about them — all quite true, of course. "Once," he said, "we were out for a route-march. One of the mules suddenly got stuck hard and fast in a bit of a morass. We pulled and tugged at him, but devil an inch could he be moved. At last we lashed on ropes and put the whole battery on to him, and after an hour's hard work the mule suddenly shot out of the mud with a loud oleaginous sort of smack; and on examining the place to ascertain how the

WAITING FOR THE ORDERS OF THE DAY.

beast had become stuck so firmly, a leech was found at the bottom of the mud, and he had been holding on to the mule all the time!" "On another occasion the mules were out grazing, and one suddenly disappeared in a deep swampy pool. To give the alarm and obtain assistance to pull the animal out occupied an hour or so. When the rescue party arrived, they could see the animal several feet below the water, at the bottom of the pool, fast in the mud up to his chest. They thought he must be dead; but no, he was not! Not to waste his time, however, he was quietly nibbling away at the weeds and things that grew around him at the bottom of the pool. When he heard the footfalls of his rescuers, he simply raised his head and moved his ears backwards and forwards, but showed no other emotion, and so he waited quietly till his deliverers were able to haul him out. This story beautifully illustrates the patient spirit of the mule under adversity!"

Refreshments on the March.

A CAMP PICKET.

Everyone carried cooked food of some kind or description in his haversack. This he munched as he went along or ate during some of the many halts that occurred. If, however, no long halt had previously been made, one for twenty min- utes or half- an-hour was usually al- lowed be- tween 11 and 12 o'clock.

The Best Way to Climb a Hill.

Most of the officers had ponies, and it is certainly much nicer getting up a hill on a pony's back, if it can be done, than on one's own pins. However, there were many places where this could not be done. The next best thing was to hang on to your pony's tail. It might not have been a dignified way of climbing a hill, but it helped you to keep your wind, and, when you reached the top of the hill, you could talk, while the others around you gasped for breath and, for the life of them, could not utter a word.

Arrival in Camp.

The camp was usually reached in the afternoon. All of us were then very busy with our various duties; some telling off sites, others looking after their men, or posting the usual sentries and pickets, or issuing the orders for the day.

HOW TO CLIMB A MOUNTAIN!

Thacker, Spink & Co., Calcutta.

These and many other details of camp life keep us all engaged for some time. The Political Officer is busy receiving deputations of Chins; and then, the safety and cleanliness of the camp being duly provided for, we gradually settle down. The coolies come trooping in an hour or so later, brought up by the rear-guard. The wood is gathered and the camp-fires are lighted, and presently our servants bring us hot cups of tea or cocoa, which, under the circumstances, are indeed grateful and comforting.

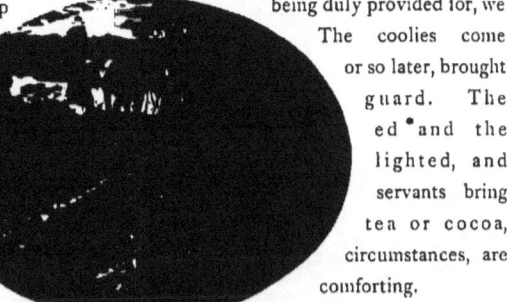

ON THE MARCH; SICK OFFICER RESTING.

The Rear-guard has a Bad Time of it.

On a few occasions when the marches were long and the paths very bad, and there were many weary hills to climb and water was scarce, the rear-guard and coolies did not reach camp till long past midnight. Some of the dhoolie-bearers would fall down the *khud* in the dark, or some of the coolies would get lost and would be brought in days after by friendly Chins, or a few sepoys would miss the way in the darkness and fall asleep in the jungle. Relief parties with lighted pine-wood torches would have to be sent out to light the belated ones into camp. On such occasions the officer commanding the rear-guard had a very unpleasant time of it. Indeed, after the first

THE FIELD HOSPITAL: THE MEDICAL OFFICER'S VISIT.

experience, he always provided himself with candles, food, blankets, and a flask full of whisky or rum, to be prepared for all contingencies. Experiences such as these, however, were happily not the rule. The rear-guard usually arrived in camp in good time.

The "dhoolies" and "Kahars."

When first advancing into the hills we had, of necessity, to camp in the deadly valleys at the foot of the hills, and here the troops and followers contracted much sickness. Men were constantly falling out on the march and had to be carried in the *dhoolies*. These latter were heavy cumbrous affairs, and, when laden, it was a matter of much difficulty carrying them up the steep hills with narrow paths that took sharp bends round precipices and slippery spurs. This made the progress very slow. The bearers, themselves a feeble lot, went sick in large numbers, and added to the difficulties. When there is any hard work to be done the *kahar* always breaks down. His favourite expression, when you request him to "*chulo*" and not delay the column, is, "I am dying!" Whenever you meet a party of *kahars*, they whine this dirge at you—"We are all dying." But it becomes monotonous, and not only fails to rouse the pity in your bosom it is intended to excite, but it

BRINGING SICK ACROSS A RIVER.

CAMP OF THE DHOOLIE-BEARERS.

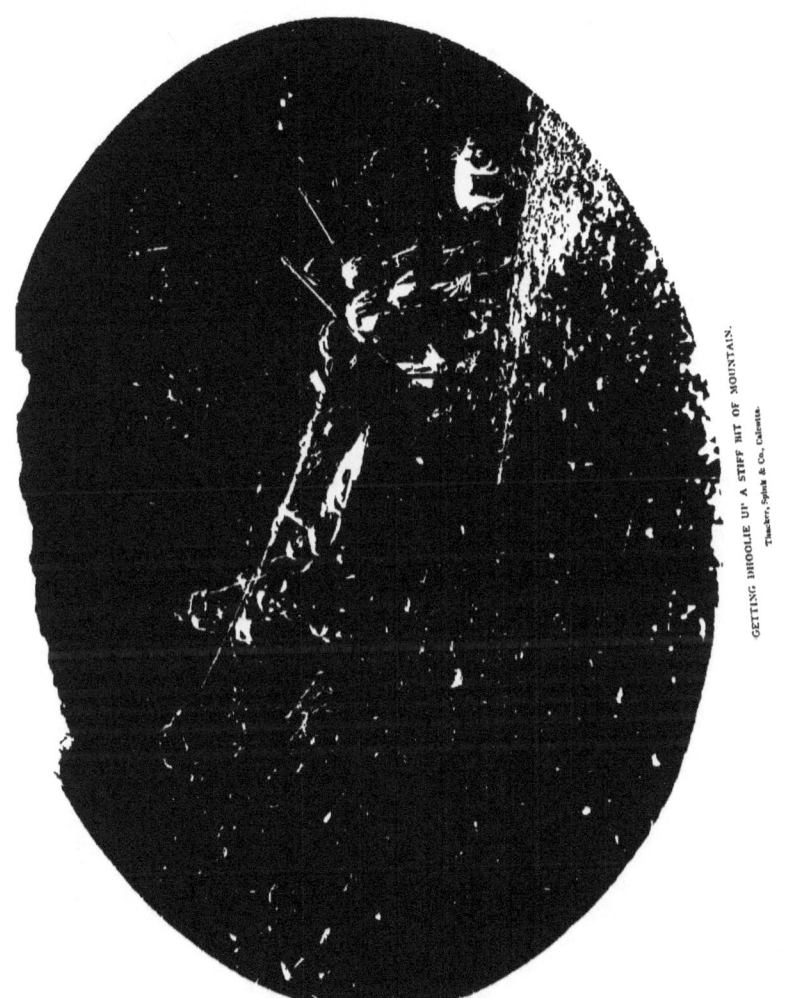

GETTING BHOOLIE UP A STIFF BIT OF MOUNTAIN.
Thacker, Spink & Co., Calcutta.

absolutely makes one very angry after a time. On arrival in camp the dying ones are as noisy as jackdaws, and snarl and wrangle over their *ghee* and *lotas*, and other equally important matters.

Our Jungle Camp.

Sometimes we had to camp in dark, dense jungles, where the air was stagnant and heavy, and where we had to cut down the trees to let in the light and air. Some of the camps were very bad; but there was no help for it. We could not go to the top of the mountain, away from the water, neither could we camp up the hill-side—usually as steep as a church-steeple; so we had to keep to the streams below. Once well into the hills, the camps were on good sites—chiefly on the hill-slopes, near villages.

VIEW IN THE BOUNGSHAY COUNTRY.

The Boungshay Country.

A MOUNTAIN CAMP—BOUNGSHAY COUNTRY.

In the Boungshay country the valleys are very narrow, and covered for the most part with dense jungle. The mountains rise to great heights. One range the troops went over was above 9,000 feet. Pine forests are not plentiful. The summits of the higher ranges are covered with dense oak-forests, from whose sombre branches hang in plenty long trailing lichen, and orchids are seen in great profusion. Generally above 4,000 feet red rhododendrons cover the hill sides. The villages are few and far-between. The paths are chiefly goat-tracks, and go straight up or down the hills. There is, no doubt, abundance of game in the country. The Chiefs are all mighty hunters, and we found their houses museums of *shikar* trophies. The Chiefs have large herds of *mythun*, which are usually allowed to roam the jungles. We also came across numbers of water-buffalo. They also have the ordinary cattle; but this is the result of their raids into Burma. In many of these southern villages there were large numbers of white hill-goats. Occasionally the Chins paid goats and *mythun* as tribute. This provided us with fresh meat for many days. Fowls and eggs were also plentiful, and paid in as tribute. The nominal tribute they had to pay was one rupee for each house. In most of the villages we were able to get oranges and plaintains. Vegetables were scarce—the only vegetable universally grown seems to be a variety of bean. In some places yams and sweet potatoes and pumpkins were also grown. Millet and Indian corn is the staple diet of the Chin. Pigs

CAMP NEAR SHUKKWA.

A CAMP IN THE BOUNGSHAY COUNTRY.

POLITICAL OFFICER INTERVIEWING CHINS.
Thacker, Spink & Co, Calcutta.

and pariah dogs abounded. Chins do not eat their dogs, as was at one time erroneously supposed; but the pig is a tit-bit reserved for all festive and state occasions.

Klung-Klung Country.

In the Klung-Klung country the valleys are broader and the hills not so high, but there is little undergrowth jungle, and the whole country abounds in beautiful pine forest, the air one breathes everywhere being delightfully fragrant and fresh.

Tashon Country.

Towards the north, in the Tashon country, the hills are very densely populated, and nearly the whole of the hill-sides have been cleared for cultivation. One meets with very little jungle anywhere, and so it is farther north. There are mighty hunters in the Klung-Klung country too, but owing to the clearing of the jungles and the densely populated valleys in the Tashon country, it is devoid of game, and the people are not great *shikaris* but great agriculturists.

TASHON COLUMN ENCAMPED AT FALAM.

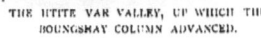

THE HTITE VAR VALLEY, UP WHICH THE HOUNGSHAY COLUMN ADVANCED.

The Country is Difficult.

Sometimes the country to be visited was

so difficult, that the guns and all animals had to be left behind at the base, and only the troops with coolies made the ex- pedition. The climbing on such occasions was ter- rible; of- ten it was a case of "holding on by your eye- lids," as the ele- gant ex- pression goes. One razor- back ridge on the Dawn Mountain in the Klung- Klung coun- try will never be forgotten by those who had to climb it. It is about the worse bit of mountain- path in the whole of the Chin Hills, and that is saying a good deal. On each side of this steep craggy ridge is a precipice of 3,000 or 4,000 feet, to look down which made one feel quite dizzy. The Chins call this break- neck spot, "The place where the dog fell down." It is the sort of place Rider Haggard might have conceived, and up which some of his bloodthirsty heroes might have had to climb in search of hidden treasure or on some other bold adven- ture.

THE GREAT SOUTHERN BEND OF THE "BOINU" (CHIEFTAIN'S BRIDE) ROUND THE "BOIPA" MOUNTAIN (THE CHIEFTAIN).

OUR FIRST VIEW OF THE BOINU RIVER BELOW SHURKWA VILLAGE.

We Receive Warlike Reports.

The reports at first

DESCENDING A BAD BIT OF MOUNTAIN PATH: THE DAWN MOUNTAINS.

Thacker, Spink & Co., Calcutta.

received were always of a more or less warlike nature, and were generally to the tune that the more distant villages would strenuously resist the advance of troops into their country. But eventually peaceful councils prevailed everywhere and the troops were received in all directions in a friendly spirit. On one occasion only did we find that they had *panjgie*-d or spiked a place with sharp bamboos. We were, however, warned of this, and the only creature that suffered was an obstinate old mule who persisted in wandering off the path, and one of his feet was run through by a *panjgie* for his trouble. When a good Samaritan of a Tommy did the animal a good turn by pulling out the spike, the ungrateful beast repaid his kindness by kicking him in the stomach. But, to be sure, there are others besides mules who display this virtue. There was, for instance, the Chin whom we treated with rum and other delicacies,

THE HIGHEST POINT REACHED BY THE HOUNGSHAY COLUMN, OVER 9,000 FEET.

ENTRANCE TO SOUTHERN HOUNGSHAY VILLAGE.

and who, before leaving camp, quietly walked off with one of our *kukries*. There too was the *sahib*, who, having no matches himself, borrowed a box from his *syce* on the march, and then swore at the man because the matches would not light.

ENTRANCE TO A TASHON VILLAGE.

We are met by the Chiefs.

The Chiefs and principal men of the village the troops were marching for, always came out several miles with presents of fowls, eggs, oranges, and gourds full of *Yu*, to meet the column. Having given in their submission, they conducted the troops to their village, near which the camp would be pitched. Later on the Chiefs would come in and pay their tribute, and discuss matters with the Political Officer.

ENTRANCE TO A YAHOW VILLAGE.

Chiefs come in to submit.

If we halted a day or two, the Chiefs of surrounding villages that we had not been able to visit from various causes, would come in with their strings of followers carrying the usual presents and give in their submission: and then they would go round and inspect the wonders to be seen in the strangers' camp. The Chin evidently does not consider that "there is a time for everything." In some camps strings of these deputations kept coming and going all day long, and sometimes at night. Often they turned up in the small hours of the morning, and sitting round the Political Officer's tent, they would shout, "*Kapa! Kapa!*" which being interpreted means, "O Father! O Father!" And they would keep on shouting till the "Father" gave them an audience. It was no use swearing at them. They did not understand that, and only "*Kapa*-d" you the louder. If an idea struck a Chin, and he wanted to impart it to the Political Offi-cer, he came to

A 'CHIN GRAVEYARD.

A CLUMP OF BAMBOOS AT AN ALTITUDE OF 6,000 FT. AT ENTRANCE TO A CHIN VILLAGE.

A midnight visit.

On one occasion we were all asleep in the verandah of a Chin house. To keep the wind out we had tied a waterproof sheet across the front of the verandah. About midnight we were all suddenly startled by the familiar "*Kapa! Kapa!*" in long drawn-out guttural tones. We sat up in our beds, and there peering over the waterproof sheet at us were a number of hideous Chin faces, with dishevelled hair, lit up by flaming pine-torches. They grinned at us and seemed to enjoy the situation. They were a deputation from a neighbouring village that had come in to submit. Owing to these little peculiarities of the Chin, we had to erect our tents well away from the Political Officer's; otherwise we were never certain of our night's repose.

LUNNOO, THE SOUTHERNMOST VILLAGE VISITED BY THE HOUNGSHAY COLUMN.

KAWYWA, THE MOST WESTERLY CHIN VILLAGE VISITED.

How we drank *Yu* at a Chief's house.

Perhaps a Chief would invite us to drink a friendly cup of *Yu* at his house. We remember one occasion of this kind. When the camp-fires were burning merrily all round and throwing a cheerful glow on the groups round each, the Chief of the village came and invited us to his mansion. It was a cold night and some preferred the warmth of the fire and their post-prandial pipes and mugs of rum. A few of the hardier ones, however, went. The Chins formed a circle round a huge *Yu* jar, and the liquor had to be sucked out of the jar through a reed in the orthodox Chin fashion, the quantity each guest had to drink being marked by a piece of stick. Each guest had to suck away till the liquid reached a certain level. To the Chin "this was nothing new," as the mule said

GOATS BROUGHT IN AS TRIBUTE.

HEAD-QUARTER CAMP AT MUNLIPI (KLUNG-KLUNG).

when it fell down the *khud* for the twentieth time. But it was a strain on the

"*Boipas*" (Chin for *sahibs*), and some felt the effects of that mild debauch next day and the day after that.

A MYTHUN PAID IN AS TRIBUTE.

Yu and its virtues.

This *Yu*, or Chin beer, varies in quality immensely. No two brews are alike. The liquor first drawn off is naturally much stronger than the subsequent liquid; for, as the beer sinks in the jar as it is drawn off through the reed, more and more water is added. This beer, when good, is not unlike inferior cider; at any rate it is refreshing and acceptable when you have nothing better to drink, especially after a long, weary, dusty march over many hills. After a time all of us took kindly to *Yu*, and, whenever a Chin deputation came in, the *Yu*

A STIFF CLIMB.

gourds were always in great request. It is intoxicating stuff too, if you imbibe too much of it, as some of us know from experience; and it is capable of giving you a head that you will remember for many a day. This is a complaint not unknown even among the most veteran Chin topers. They frequently came to our camp for medicine to cure their heads—but they put it down to fever! Strange how we all—savage and civilized alike—try to find plausible excuses for our little failings.

VILLAGE OF KLUNG-KLUNG—CAPITAL OF THE TRIBE OF THE SAME NAME.

Rainy weather experiences.

When the weather was threatening or rainy, we usually occupied a portion of the houses in a village, the owners doubling up with the others. The houses, however, required a good deal of cleaning up before they were habitable. A Chin house is usually chock-full of rubbish of all kinds, chiefly huge wicker-baskets. Then a plank or two have to be taken out of the sides to let in the light and air: for there are no windows in a Chin house, which is perfectly dark inside. The roof and walls are black

VILLAGE OF MUNLIPI (KLUNG-KLUNG).

with cobwebs and to the general inside of a is not a place, is lively for it swarms min of all pigs and my- the house. The the fowls and dogs with the humans. smoke and add gloom. The Chin house cheerful though it enough, usually with ver- sorts. The *thun* live under little piggies and share the house

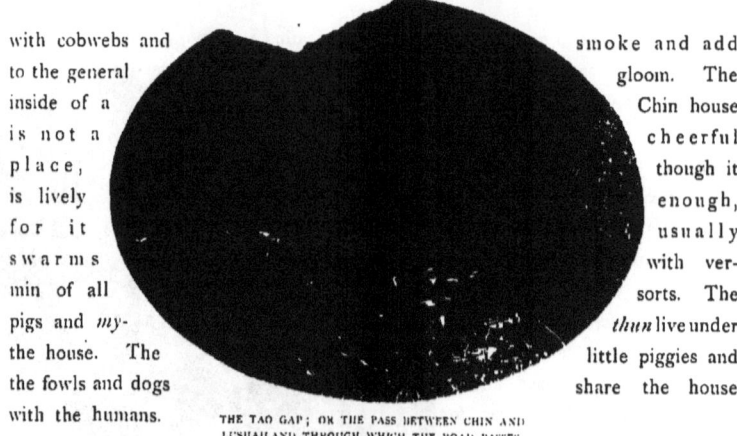

THE TAO GAP; OR THE PASS BETWEEN CHIN AND LUSHAILAND THROUGH WHICH THE ROAD PASSES.

The Baby cries.

The verandah is the best part of the house and we usually slept in it, leaving

THE TAO MOUNTAIN.

the family undisturbed in the rest of the house. But they had not the same consideration for us; for about two or three o'clock in the morning the baby

MEETING OF THE TWO COLUMNS AT TAO: SENDING OFF THE NEWS BY HELIO.

Thacker, Spink & Co., Calcutta.

would begin to cry, babies, and the would try to ing what was Chin lullaby, what sound- a dismal certainly put sleep, what- might have had as is the wont of Chin mamma quiet it by sing- meant for a no doubt, but ed to us like croaking and an end to our ever effect it on the baby.

We visit a Chief in his house.

The Political Offi- cer usually visits every Chief in his house, accompanied by one or two officers, with a small escort of sepoys and a party of friendlies. Let me picture such a scene. On entering the house the party is followed by a crowd of odor- ous Chins, who troop in from the neighbouring houses, some smoking strong smelling rank to- bacco in long bam- boo pipes. A Chin house usually con- tains three large rooms. The first is a sort of sitting-room, open in front, where guests are received. The walls of this room are usually decorated with trophies

A JHOOM, OR CHIN CLEARING FOR CULTIVATION.

THE BLUE MOUNTAIN.

of the hunt and of raids. The second is the sleeping-room, in one corner of which there is a large fire-place round which the inmates sleep: and the third is the apartment where all the cooking is done, and where the family generally lives. These rooms open into one another by round holes with a kind of sliding-door to close each. To enter the front room you have to ascend a raised platform which occupies the whole of one side of the enclosed yard in front of every house. On this raised platform or balcony the family sit during the day to talk, work, sleep, or drink *Yu*. The ground beneath the house, where the pigs and cattle are kept, is churned into thick black mire, and the yard in front is often not much better. In spite of all this the Chins are a very healthy race. In the front yard you will observe the raid-trophies that every Chin erects when he has made a successful foray. A raid trophy is looked upon as a badge of prowess in war. They correspond to the V.C.'s of our army. These trophies consist of a rudely carved board which is fixed to some uprights driven into the ground. Long bamboos are attached to the posts, and from the drooping ends of the bamboos are suspended rudely shaped emblems of birds and reptiles and

A CHIN BRIDGE

WITH THE ADVANCE-GUARD: "DUSHMEN HAI, SAHIB!"

WE VISIT A CHIN CHIEF: OUR RECEPTION.
Thacker, Spink & Co. Calcutta.

other strange things. When the wind sweeps up the mountain-side, the bamboos sway about and these wooden devices strike against one another, and at night they sound like the rattling of dead men's bones, as if they were coming to life again to cry out for vengeance against their murderers. But we have wandered from our visit to the Chief. Let us go back to the house. In the front or reception-room is a raised sort of dais in every big house, running across the whole breadth of the house. On this the guests usually sit and talk. We enter and sit down on this. Mats or *mythun* skins are spread for our feet. The Chief and other headmen of the village squat round us, and the rest of the crowd deposit themselves wherever they can find room. The Chief or his wife, the latter smoking the usual pipe, now comes forward with a gourd of *Yu* and a drinking vessel of lacquer, and the liquor is poured out and handed to the "*Boipas*" or *sahibs*, who, to show that there is no ill-feeling, must drink the proffered cup. Even if you dislike the stuff, you must drink it, and look pleased, and say, "*Atah*!" which means "excellent." A Chin thinks you a poor creature indeed, if you can't appreciate the qualities of his *Yu*. Then the usual

A STIFF DESCENT.

CHIN DEPUTATION WAITING TO RECEIVE COLUMN.

presents of fowls, eggs, plantains and sugar-cane are produced. Having drunk and eaten a plantain or two, the talking begins. This is accompanied by much gesticulation and shouting. They are a very excitable lot and

ON THE MARCH: RECEIVING THE SUBMISSION OF A VILLAGE.

cannot speak without jactitation. The *Yu* cups circulate freely among the crowd, who to save time suck in the liquor from the gourds. If a *Yu* jar is on tap, which is usually the case, the Chins take it by turns to sit by it and drinking a

GALLERY OF CHIN BEAUTY WATCHING ARRIVAL OF COLUMN.

suck in the liquor through the reed, each pint or so. The liquor is very gradually and deliberately swallowed. It is rolled about in the mouth and then allowed to trickle down the throat, so as to give the drinker the full benefit and bouquet of the liquor. *Yu* is usually prepared from fermented Indian corn and millet or other grain.

RECEIVING A CHIN DEPUTATION ON THE MARCH.

NO. 2 STOCKADE AT FOOT OF CHIN HILLS.

A Chin takes the keenest interest in every instrument of war. The edges of our swords are examined to see if they are sharp. He gives a little sniff of

POLITICAL OFFICER RECEIVING SUBMISSION OF TASHON CHIEFS ON THE MARCH.

contempt, if he finds they are not as keen as razors. Their own *dahs* and daggers are always kept beautifully sharp. Fire-arms are what always fetch the Chins. Their eager admiring looks, when our revolvers are produced, indicate that they would give a good deal to be the possessors of such weapons themselves. Taking a shot-gun or revolver to pieces, or shooting out the cartridges, is as good as a play to a Chin audience. Their exclamations of wonder and astonishment are amusing to witness. The wo- men - folk peep from behind the door or through chinks in the boards, and, no doubt, believe LITTLE CHIN GIRLS WATCHING ARRIVAL OF TROOPS. that the white strangers are performing some fearful feats of magic. The men are always keen to see some shots fired. We give them an exhibition, but not always with success.

However, to smash an egg with a shot-gun at fifty feet is a performance which raises you tremendously in the estimation of a Chin!

Our field-glasses next come in for a share of their admiration. Looking through the magnifying end and then through the opposite end produces ludicrous bewilderment; and causing fire by magnifying glasses is also a source of endless astonishment. These wonders we have to exhibit to each one in turn till the besieging crowd is satisfied. More talking then goes on, and the lady of the house produces a flask of choice tobacco-juice, decanted from her own pipe-bowl, which she politely offers us. Our interpreter tells her we smoke tobacco but never drink the juice, although we are highly flattered at the compliment she has paid us in offering us the elixir. This liquid is prepared by the women of the household in their pipes. Every woman and girl smokes a pipe, at the lower end of which is a chamber containing water, into which the nicotine and liquid from the pipe bowl percolate. When the solution is of sufficient strength, it is decanted into little gourds. This liquid is largely consumed by Chins. They are always taking nips from these flasks,

THE BELLE OF THE VILLAGE.

A FRIENDLY CHAT WITH CHINS.

nearly every Chin carrying a supply of the nauseous-looking stuff. Why they are not poisoned by it is a mystery. On long marches and on all festive occasions, these tobacco- bottles are just as much in requisi- tion as the Yu jars. The Chin ought, therefore, to be the boonest of boon com- panions, as those two great virtues, namely, the capacity for con- suming much liquor and much tobacco, he possesses in the highest degree! When we have declined the proffered honour, the tobacco-juice is passed round to the elders in the crowd; everyone takes a sip, and the bottle is handed back to the lady.

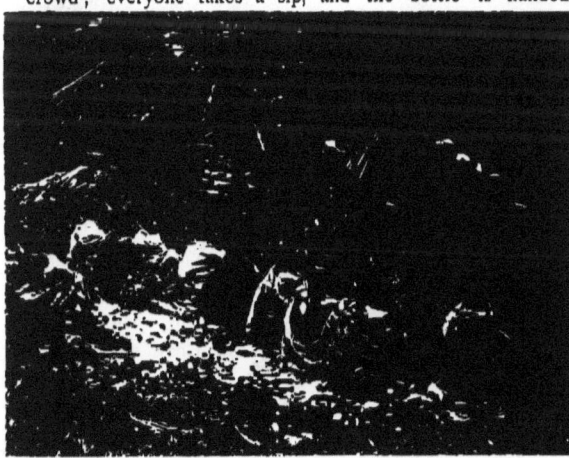

THE POLITICAL OFFICER RECEIVING A DEPUTATION OF CHINS IN CAMP.

CHINS WAITING TO SEE THE POLITICAL OFFICER

By this time the Political Officer has managed to make the Chief understand what he wants done. Our business end- ed, we rise up and, cautiously picking our way over the creaking and rickety boards of the balcony, we leave the house and return to camp, and so ends our visit.

Captives refuse to be released.

In releasing Burmese captives from the Chins, among the difficulties that cropped up was this curious one—the captives refused to be released! These were chiefly girls and boys, who had been carried away from Burma when very young. They had thus grown up as Chins and knew no language but Chin, and had come to look upon the Chins as their own people. Such captives kicked and bit and scratched and cried, and no doubt also swore, when the Political Officer attempted to release them and give them to their fond parents. Such is human nature! Sometimes the Chiefs had to be put in the Quarter-Guard and kept there, till the villagers produced the captives demanded.

OBTAINING INFORMATION.

A funeral party disturbed.

In one of the columns a funeral-party was performing the last rites for a dead comrade, when the Chins, objecting to one of their fields being used as a burial-ground, hurled a volley of stones at the burial-party. They were, however, soon put to flight, and the interment completed without further interference.

ENTRANCE TO A CHIEF'S HOUSE.

THE WUNTHO CHIEF'S HOUSE (KUNGKLUNG). THE LARGEST AND BEST HOUSE IN THE WHOLE OF THE CHIN HILLS.
Thacker Spink & Co, Calcutta.

THE IMAGE OF WAR; OR, SERVICE ON THE CHIN HILLS.   55

News spread rapidly.

It is wonderful how quickly news get about in these hills. On one occasion we heard that an important Chief we wanted to capture was in a certain village. All plans were carefully made, and the village was surrounded by troops at daybreak, and the whole place searched. The missing man, however, was not found, but the village chiefs and elders were discovered at that hour of the morning still sitting up and carousing over their Yu jars, and they pretended to know nothing of the fugitive. We could only exclaim, "Better luck next time!" as a dashing and gallant young officer sadly remarked, when he captured what he believed to be a large party of hostile Chins, but discovered to his disgust, on bringing them into camp, that they were only friendly Chin coolies who were coming

CHIN CHILDREN.

A CHIN HOUSE.

in to carry rations for the column, and with the discovery all the visions of D.S.O's and other honours faded from his sight!

Chins and rupees and barter.

THE FALAM WAR-CHIEF'S HOUSE.

CHIN HOUSES, SHOWING PLATFORMS AND PALISADES.

Everywhere we found the Chins would have nothing to say to the rupee with the Queen's head. The only coin they appeared to consider genuine was the Empress-rupee: though how or why they got hold of this idea it is difficult to say. Probably the first coins they handled were rupees with the Empress superscription on them. Small silver coins too were at a discount. Sometimes Chins brought in Queen-rupees which they offered to exchange for Empress ones, and, as an inducement, they threw in a few dozen eggs or a bunch of plantains with each coin—offers which the men were not slow to accept. Others offered four four-anna pieces or two eight-anna bits, with a handful of copper coin thrown in, in exchange for Empress rupees. The Chin idea of the value of money is very vague. He will no doubt soon learn better. A *thanka* or rupee is his

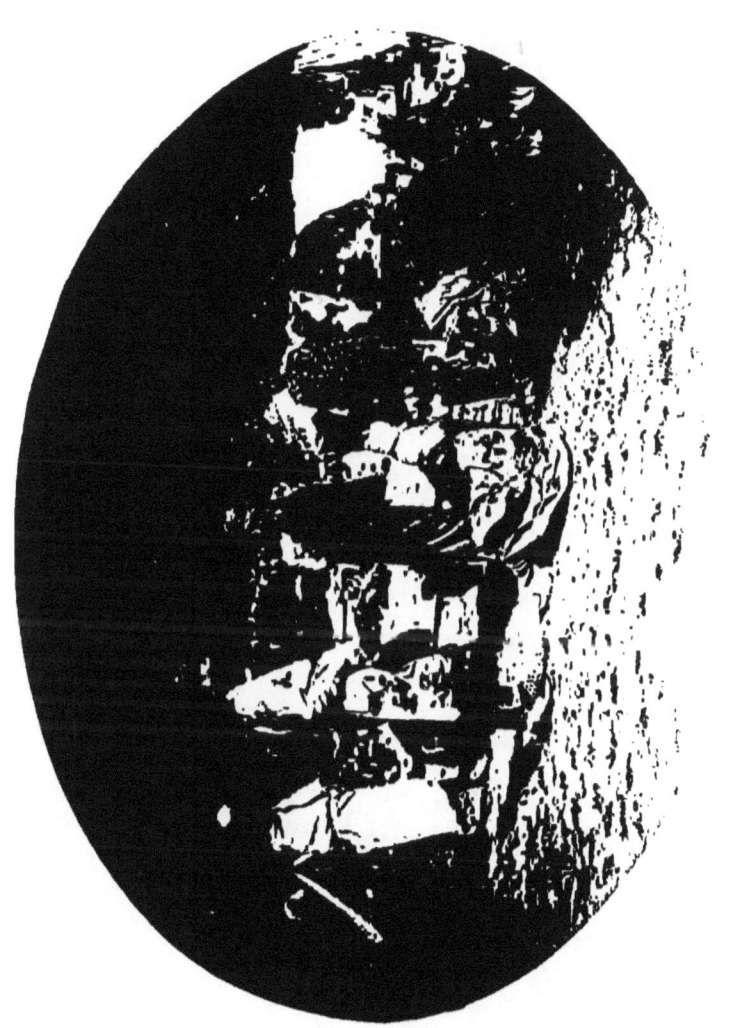

standard for everything he has to sell, whether it be a chicken, or a basket of beans, or a bunch of plantains, or a few eggs.

RAID-TROPHIES AT TUNZAN, PUT UP IN HONOUR OF THE MURDER OF LIEUT. STEWART.

The Chin likes a gamey egg.

On one occasion the Chins sold us some eggs, and on breaking a few we found them addled. These were thrown away; but the Chins carefully picked them up and put them into their bags, reserving them, no doubt, as *bonnes bouches* for future use!

Another time the guileless Chin took us in completely. All eggs they brought in were dropped into a basin of water to test them. So in the usual manner one day the servant bought a batch of eggs after testing them in the water. But imagine his disgust when he afterwards found that the Chin had boiled the eggs—which were all bad—and so they had sunk in the water and deceived him!

The Chin is not a fool.

The Chin is not such a fool as he looks. He has been known to sell to Burmans and others on the frontier solid slabs of beeswax, which the purchasers afterwards discovered to be straw or mud covered over with a layer of wax! Sometimes they have received a

A CHIN CHIEF AND HIS WIFE IN GALA COSTUME.

Roland for an Oliver in the shape of silvered copper coin. But on such occasions they have gone to the Civil Officer with the false coin and he has usually replaced it with good coin, and so *they* at all events have never suffered.

The Chin Ladies.

When we first came up into these hills, there were many reports regarding the scanty clothing worn by the Chin women. We have now pretty nearly penetrated every corner of these hills, but we have never come across the Chin ladies "vot hadn't got nodings on." The story about the females who only wore a piece of board is quite mythical. On the contrary, the Chin ladies dress very decently indeed, as a reference to the pictures will show. They are, however, a dirty and ugly race as a whole. The Tashon women were the only ones we came across who went about with their bosoms uncovered.

The Boung-shays.

The whole of the Chins, from the Tashons and Yahows in the North to the Lunnoos and others in the south, may be classed as Boung-shays. This is a Burmese term applied to the Chins who wear their hair dressed in a knot in

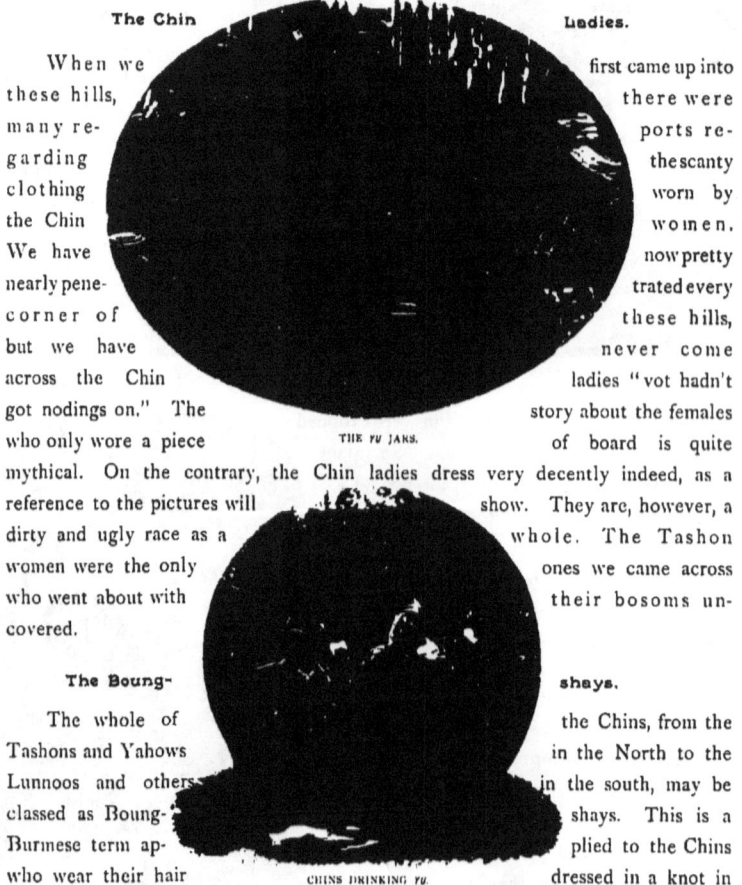

THE YU JARS.

CHINS DRINKING YU.

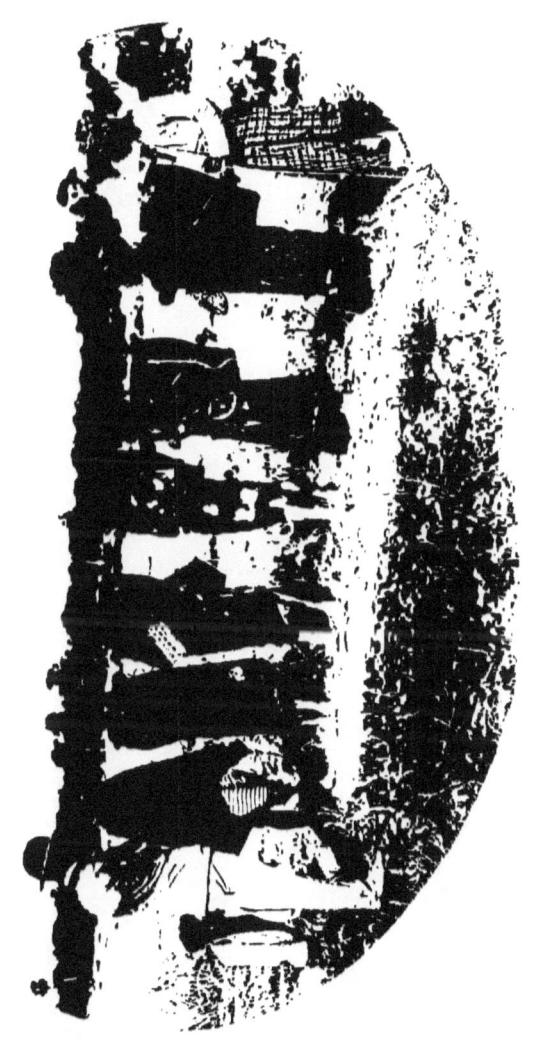

the front of their heads, the knot being rolled round with a strip of cloth. This form of head-dress is affected by all the great tribes mentioned above. The Siyins and Kanhows farther north wear their hair made up into a knot at the back of the head like a small *chignon*. The Siyins in addition ornament their heads with two small plaits worn above each temple. This manner of head-dress gives these two tribes a much less manly appearance than the hill-men of the south.

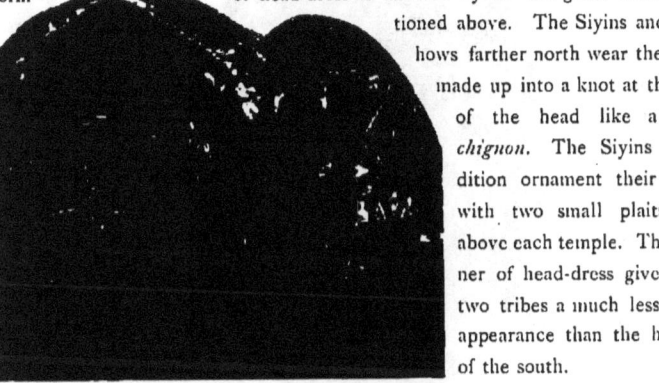

MAKING FRIENDS WITH THE CHINS.

How three old witches put out a fire.

On one occasion we were quartered in a village. We had had a big fire, round which we had spent the evening, and at the usual hour we had all turned into our beds in a Chin house. After some time when all sounds had died out, three old hags, to whom the house we were occupying evidently belonged, cautiously crept out of the darkness and sat down round the smouldering fire. Their idea, apparently, was to put out the fire, lest a wind should spring up at night and blow the sparks about and set the village in flames. Each ancient dame had a vessel of water with her. But apprehensive, no doubt, that if they threw the whole of the water suddenly on the fire, it would produce a noise and disturb the *boipas*, and they

AMUSING THE CHINS.

would thus incur their displeasure, the old beldames took mouthfuls of water and very gently squirted it on to the smouldering embers. The jets of water were aimed with great precision, and very soon they succeeded in putting out the fire without the least noise. Then with a croak of satisfaction they disappeared again into the darkness. We quietly watched the show from our beds, and very comical the whole thing appeared.

The Chins and their spittoons.

From long continued practice the Chin is very expert in aiming with his mouth. From their habit of constantly chewing or smoking rank tobacco, their salivary secretions are always very profuse. They have no spittoons, but the cracks in the floors of their houses answer just as well. The unerring way they aim is quite wonderful to watch. When a Chin sits down to talk to you, he always selects a spot near which there is a convenient crack!

CHIN WOMEN SMOKING.

How the Chin shaves.

We once came upon a Chin engaged in shaving his child's head. The hair was knotted into lumps with dirt. The shaving was done with a piece of hoop-iron finely sharp-ened. To facili- tate the process, the operator every now and

HAKA CHIEFS AND THEIR SISTERS.

again expectorated on the child's head and rubbed the spittle and dirt up into a

The Image of War; or, Service on the Chin Hills.

kind of lather, and then went on with the operation. The rest of the family sat round looking on admiringly at the skill of the operator!

Legend of the White Men.

In the Klung-Klung country we heard a curious legend regarding one of the villages. The story runs that years and years ago a party of white strangers suddenly appeared on the hills, defeating the hill-men wherever they met them; but eventually some of them settled down in the village of Shurn-gen. Here they lived at peace with their neighbours for nine years, and then disappeared as suddenly as they came. Near this village is a cave in which relics of the strange visitors are still said to be kept, which the Chins greatly venerate. We were, unfortunately, unable to visit this interesting village. The Chins say that before leaving the

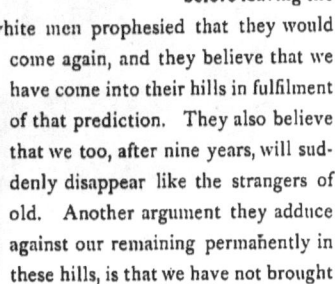

THE ONLY BURMESE CAPTIVE RELEASED BY THE TASHON COLUMN, AND HER GALLANT RESCUER.

white men prophesied that they would come again, and they believe that we have come into their hills in fulfilment of that prediction. They also believe that we too, after nine years, will suddenly disappear like the strangers of old. Another argument they adduce against our remaining permanently in these hills, is that we have not brought

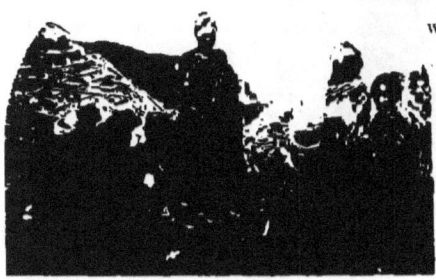

PURCHASING EGGS FROM CHINS.

our women-folk with us. "Man," they say, "cannot live without women; and so these strangers too must soon return to their own country."

A Legend of Falam.

Before the present village was built, the Tashon capital was at Old Falam, about a mile west of the present metropolis. The old village is overhung by a frowning rocky mountain, to the projecting crags of which the Chins attribute demon shapes and forms. The mountain is, therefore, called the "Beluma." We, however, failed to discover in any of the rocks the demon shapes attributed to them; but we were told it required a good deal of *Yu* to enable one to see these strange things properly—and that was probably true. From a cave amid these crags a beautiful female appeared when someone was to die in the village. At first she appeared but infrequently; but after a time the beautiful damsel's visits became very frequent, and in alarm the Tashons abandoned the place, and built the fine new village of Falam, since which time they have enjoyed uninterrupted prosperity.

HAKA BELLES.

MINLAYDAUNG CHINS.

FALAM.

UNIV. OF
CALIFORNIA

THE OCCUPATION OF FALAM: THE COLUMN ENTERING THE CAPITAL.

Thacker, Spink & Co., Calcutta.

A Chat about the Chin Friendlies.

The Political [Officer had with him] a party of friendly [Chins, mostly chiefs] or sons of chiefs. [To distinguish] them from other [Chins they wore a] strip of red cloth [round their hair.] From this cir[cumstance they] were known in [the columns as] *lalpuggri - wal*[las]. They were also known un[der the various] designations of ["Chin police,"] "P. O.'s body-[guard," "irregu]lars," "friendlies," [and "Chin militia."] They accompanied all [the expeditions, and] often rendered very [useful and important] service. They were a fine [lot of men, well set-up] and sturdy, and one or two were remarkably handsome. They were excellent foragers; and in the matter of drink they were a match for any man in these hills. They generally took the deputations, that came in to submit, under their wing, and introduced them to the Political Officer — and consumed most of the *Yu*.

Pork they had galore, for every deputation brought in several pigs, sometimes alive and squeaking, and sometimes roasted whole and skewered on a bamboo. Their method of killing

A HOUNGSHAY CHIEF IN COMPLETE WAR-PAINT.

THE WUNTOO CHIEFS AND THEIR HOUSEHOLD—THESE CHIEFS ARE GREAT NIMRODS.

a pig was as follows. The struggling, squealing animal is held down by two men, while a third takes the sharp bamboo skewer he wears in his hair and deliberately introduces it into the animal's chest, feeling his way, as it were, as he penetrates deeper. Having gone far enough, he proceeds to work the skewer about till he pierces the heart. In the meantime the wretched pig has been making the place re-echo with his death-screams. As the skewer does its work, the noise becomes fainter and yet more faint, and at last, after a quarter of an hour's suffering, piggy bids a long farewell to the little joys his kind can know in this world. The great object of the Chin is not to lose a drop of the

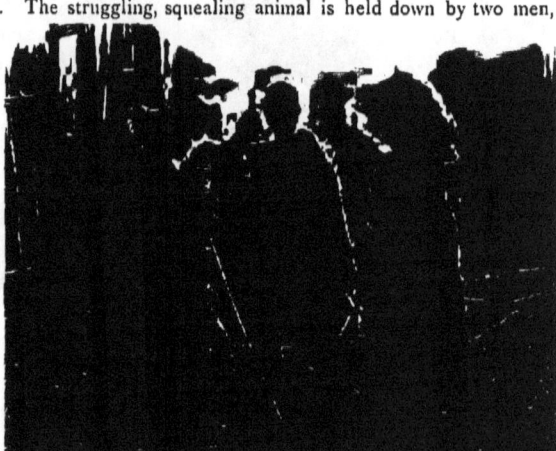

CHINS IN MONSOON COSTUME.

HEAD-QUARTER CAMP AT FALAM (TASHON).

The Image of War; or, Service on the Chin Hills. 65

blood. The entrails are then removed, and the animal is roasted whole on a big fire in his skin. He is then cut up and distributed; and the relish with which the Chins fall to on the roast flesh reminds one of the delightful story of Elia's Chinese swine-herd and the roast pig.

Lots of drink.

The Chin militia had a high old time of it all through. The *Yu* was unlimited, and at almost every village they had a drinking-bout. Rollicking by nature, they delighted in a lark so long as it was not at their own expense. We

IN THE CAMP OF THE FRIENDLIES.

were often much amused by the pranks they played on their fellow-tribesmen. Sometimes they came and sat with us round our fire, and with a few nods and grunts and motions of the hands we were able to carry on quite an interesting conversation. They picked up most of our names and rattled them off. If a Chin wishes to express his pleasure, he embraces you or strokes you gently. We had sometimes to submit

THREE GENERATIONS OF CHINS.

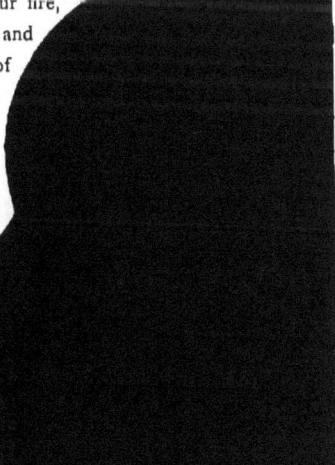

PREPARING THEIR FOOD.

to this ordeal. The embracing is embarrassing, especially if the gentleman who is so demonstrative is a bit high, as they invariably are! When you visit a Chin

A YAHOW HOUSE.

house, the old ladies too, but not the young ones unfortunately, stroke you to show their admiration for the white men.

Their funny names. Their gunpowder, bullets, and guns.

Some of these Chiefs had very funny-sounding names. The reader would call them indecent, if they were written down here. They were all excellent shots. A Chin never failed to bring down a *mythun* at the first shot, while our men took many shots, and even then the animal sometimes escaped. All these Chins are armed with old Tower flint-locks. They make their own gunpowder. We

LONGLER CHINS (KLUNG-KLUNG.)

frequently passed the sulphur-factories of villages: these consisted of wooden troughs or wicker-baskets chock-full of a large variety of bean, sunk in the streams; and from the decomposition of these beans they get their sulphur. We could

HAKA CHIEFS.

always tell when we were approaching these places, by the smells that assailed us.

The Chins are not particular what they use as bullets: pieces of telegraph-wire, pebbles, or bits of iron beaten into squares answer their purposes just as well. The barrels of their guns are what they value most. Most of the other parts they make themselves. The Chiefs' guns are usually very beautifully lacquered.

They are big feeders.

These "friendlies" were great feeders; and so, indeed, are all Chins. They were always eating. They put away a large quantity of food three times a day regularly. On the march, when we halted, we would often see them spread out a huge cloth, on which they would pile up a mountain of boiled millet and a mass of boiled eggs, with great junks of boiled or roast pork. Round this pile they would sit, and soon demolish it. Then a copious draught of water, and they were ready for anything.

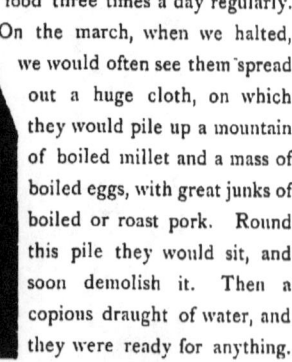

GROUP OF SIYIN CHINS.

The Tashons are the most civilized.

Of all the Chins, the Tashons are the most civilized. In the houses of their Chiefs we found oil-lamps made of earthenware—things we had never come across in any other village. The Chins, as a rule, sit round their fires, and that is the only illumination they have in their soot-begrimed houses. Round these fires, too, they hold their drinking orgies.

CAPT. KENDALL INTERVIEWING KANHOW CHIEFS.

Their midnight orgies.

These nocturnal orgies were accountable for many things, and once they came near involving an escort of sepoys in a battle royal, but for the prompt action of the Political Offi- cer. He was re- turning to a post with a small escort of ten sepoys and his body- guard of friend- lies. He arrived at a large village, where he had to pass the night. As usual, he occupied the Chief's house. The event, of course, was made the occasion for a big drink. The Chief and his people and the friendlies drank deeply and freely, sitting round the fire. At first they were a most convivial party, and everything went on smoothly; but, as the stuff rose to their heads, they began to discuss and argue about many matters, and then words rose high and finally they fell to blows. The villagers were becoming very excited, and very little more would have induced them to rush for their arms and make an attack on the Officer and his sepoy escort. The former, who was asleep, or had been trying to sleep, in an adjoining room, rushed out on hearing the noise and,

THE POLITICAL OFFICER AND HIS "FRIENDLIES," OR CHIN MILITIA.

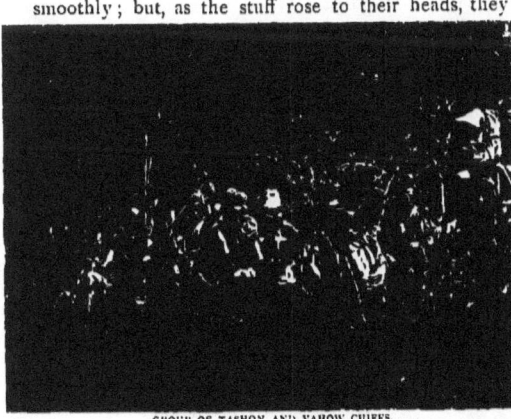

GROUP OF TASHON AND YAHOW CHIEFS.

grasping the situation, promptly collared the malcontents and placed them under guard for the rest of the night. It was an unpleasant situation. However, he kept the Chiefs well under his eye all night, and they were retained as hostages for the good behaviour of the rest of the village, till the little party left early next morning. The night's escapade, however, had resulted in not a few broken heads.

A "friendly" takes the law into his own hands.

One of the friendlies had a grievance against the Chief of a certain village. It appeared that a long time ago he had gone to the offending village to purchase some goats. But the Chief had eased him of his money and guns, and shown him the way back to his own village—but without the goats. When the column reached this village, the Chief as usual came to the camp to pay his respects. The aggrieved friendly believed his opportunity had now come to have vengeance. As soon as the Chief came into camp, the friendly sprang on him and seized and bound him hand and foot. This caused the greatest consternation among the Chief's followers, who bounded up the hill like

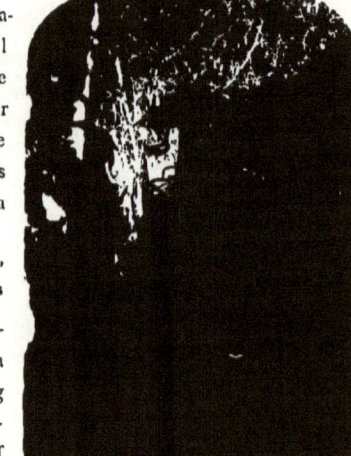

TUNNELLED ENTRANCE TO A HOUNGSHAY VILLAGE.

CHIN BREAST-WORK ON A MOUNTAIN PATH.

OFFICERS' QUARTERS, HAKA.
Thacker, Spink & Co., Calcutta.

so many antelopes. They thought it was some deep-laid plot to compass their destruction. When we learned what all the excitement was about, the Political Officer had the utmost difficulty by dint of much shouting and yelling in calming the fears of the runaways, and inducing them to trust themselves to the camp again. Their Chief was at once set

OUR ARTIST SHOWING A SKETCH TO CHINS, WHICH THEY PROMPTLY RUBBED OUT!

free. The friendly who had taken the law into his own hands in this way, and who no doubt thought he had a perfect right to do so, was promptly put into durance vile, and, being a high and mighty Chief in his own right, and a trusty policeman by the grace of the Political Officer, this was great ignominy. However, a cold night under the stern eye of the British sentry no doubt brought home to his mind the fact that, if he had any disputes, he must take

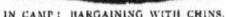

IN CAMP: BARGAINING WITH CHINS.

them to the white Chief for settlement, as that was in future to be the new order of things in the land. Subsequently the dispute was arranged to the satisfaction of both parties.

They object to being sketched.

The Chins are very superstitious and believe in the evil eye. They strongly objected to being sketched. Our artist

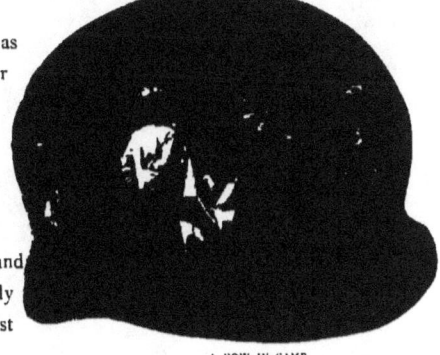

A ROW IN CAMP.

once made a very beautiful sketch of two fine-looking Chins and handed his book to the men, imagining that they would admire their own portraits. They looked at it for a while, turning it round in all directions, and finally, when they grasped what it meant, one of the men quietly moistened his finger with the tip of his tongue and smeared the sketch out, before the disgusted artist could stop him.

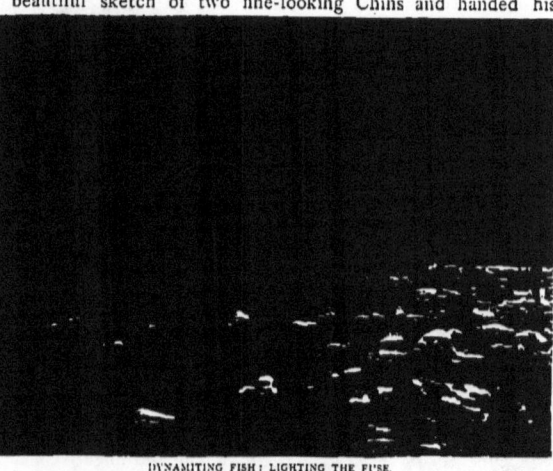

DYNAMITING FISH: LIGHTING THE FUSE.

Then with a smile that was child-like and bland he handed back the book and simply said, "*Atahlo*," which means "bad."

The Camera alarms them.

Neither did they like being photographed. When they were told what it meant,

DYNAMITING FISH: THE EXPLOSION.

they scampered away in great fright like an alarmed flock of sheep. The only way was to take them unawares. Once, in a distant village, we had erected the camera and arranged everything nicely, but, when the shutter was snapped, the Chins fled in all directions, believing it to be some kind of diabolical machine ; and nothing would induce them to approach the camera again.

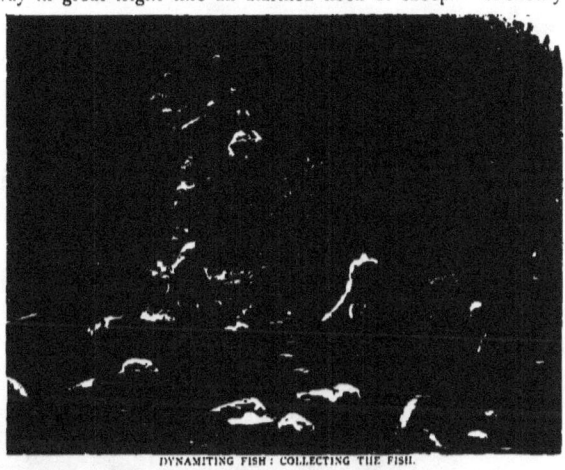

DYNAMITING FISH : COLLECTING THE FISH.

In other places, however, where the people were not so wild, the image on the ground glass was a source of great wonder and admiration to them.

Stockades and Tunnels.

In the Boungshay country all the villages have stockades and tunnelled entrances. The villages are

DYNAMITING FISH : EVERYONE HELPS TO GATHER THE FISH.

usually on the slopes of hills, rarely at a lower altitude than three or four thousand feet, and their water-supply is brought down from the springs above by wooden aqueducts. The Klung-Klungs usually have their villages perched on the summit of ridges, and trust to their inaccessible position for their defence. They therefore have to go down for their water. Except Falam, none of the Tashon or Yahow villages have defences of any kind. The houses of the great tribes are all very substantially built of fir and pine-wood. As you approach the Lushai border, however, the houses are of a more temporary nature, and are mainly built of bamboo and grass.

The most powerful Tribes.

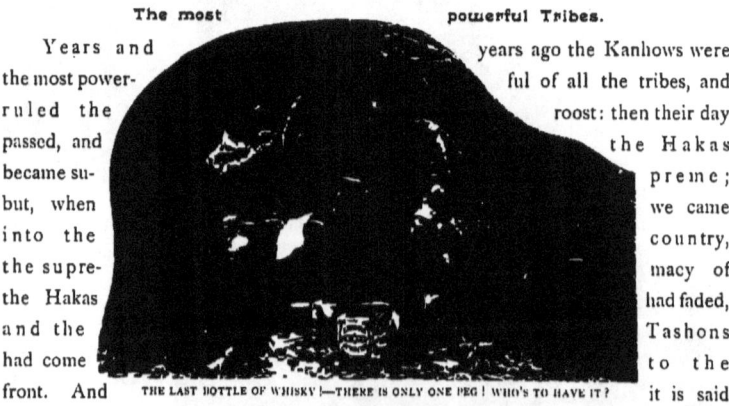

THE LAST BOTTLE OF WHISKY!—THERE IS ONLY ONE PEG! WHO'S TO HAVE IT?

Years and years ago the Kanhows were the most power- ful of all the tribes, and ruled the roost: then their day passed, and the Hakas became su- preme; but, when we came into the country, the supre- macy of the Hakas had faded, and the Tashons had come to the front. And it is said that, had we not come, the Tashons in turn would have given place to the Yahows, who at the time were carrying everything before them. Now let us hope the hatchet will be buried, and peace and good order will reign over all the land.

They are Suspicious.

The Chins are very suspicious. Often, when they came to sit by our fire, we offered them food. They would take the morsel in the tips of their fingers and smell it very cautiously. Then they would turn it round and smell it again, much as a monkey would do. Then they would break it and smell it again. After that it was very cautiously applied to the tip of the tongue, and, if it did not suit

EXAMINING CAPTURED ARMS.

Thacker, Spink & Co., Calcutta.

their refined palates, they screwed up their faces, spat on the ground, and handed the stuff back with the intimation that it was "*Atahlo*"—bad! Sugar, *gour*, salt, and rum were what they mainly appreciated.

Rockets.

Sometimes we had to send up signal-rockets to communicate with other columns. These made a profound impression on the savages. The roar of astonishment that burst from them as they watched the rockets hissing up into the heavens, was like the sound of many waters. They believed we accomplished all this by the agency of Nats.

Dynamiting Fish.

AFTERNOON TEA IN CAMP.

Dynamiting fish also greatly fetched them. "You throw something into the water; then follows a little splash, and behold! the fish come up dead in numbers. How simple! If they could only do that, how much trouble it would save them! Here were these strangers who secured all the best fish in a few minutes without the least trouble, while they took days and days to catch a few fish in spite of all their traps and snares." So thought our friends the Chins.

The Nat and the Godfather.

The Chins are demon—or Nat-worshippers. Each household has got its own special Nat. On one occasion a woman who did not exactly know who the father of her child was, and was consequently uncertain under the protection of whose Nat her brat would come, thought she would settle the matter satisfactorily by asking the Political Officer to become the Nat-father of her child! From a Chin point of view, we were told, this was considered a great compliment.

The Chin Character.

The Chin appears to be affectionate and domesticated enough, when occasion requires. We have often come across a fond Chin father nursing the baby; and they have frequently come into camp with babies tied on their backs. Mr. Macnabb thinks "they are a queer and singular race, combining many of the

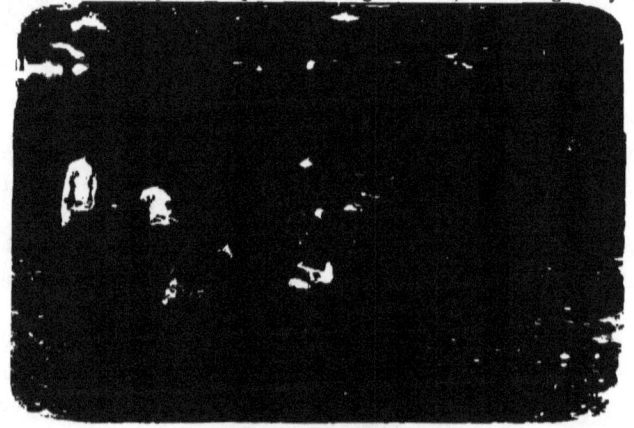

BURMESE CAPTIVES RELEASED FROM THE CHINS.

more attractive qualities of the Burman with the deceit and vindictiveness of the Pathan. On the whole, however, they are a manly race and an independent one, and, as such, command respect." The population of the country is very considerable. Indeed, the number of inhabitants in these hills quite astonished us.

The Chin as a Bargainer.

Bargaining with a Chin required a good deal of diplomacy. It was often a source of great fun to us. They were very unconfiding, and would on no account part with anything till the *thanka* or rupee was placed in their hands. With one hand the Chin would hold the article he had for sale concealed in his basket, or

OFFICERS BARGAINING WITH CHINS.

Thacker, Spink & Co., Calcutta.

under his dirty rags. This he would partly disclose and let you look at from a distance, but not handle. The other hand he held out to the intending purchaser; and, when the latter deposited the coin therein, then he would hand over the article to you and not before. If the amount one offered did not satisfy him, he simply gave a little sneeze of contempt and politely turned his back on you. The children of the hills, however, always set a very high value on their own goods. They considered a fowl or a few eggs good enough to give in exchange for anything you had. What, however, had the greatest value in their eyes were our brass uniform-buttons, which they were very keen on possessing. These they made into necklaces for themselves or their wives. With a ton or so of brass buttons one could get on very comfortably on these hills. At first empty bully-beef and biscuit-tins had a certain value in their eyes; and they gave beans or yams in exchange. But the 'cute savages soon found out they could get these things for nothing by waiting. For if they did not buy them, the troops had to throw them away, as they could not carry empty tins about. As soon as the column marched out of camp, the Chins, who hung about the outskirts, would rush in and gather up all the rubbish; and eventually they would set the camp on fire. Somebody suggested they did this for sanitary reasons! But we suspect it was done to get rid of all traces of the hated strangers from the neighbourhood of their villages.

VILLAGE OF SHURKWA, AFTERWARDS BURNT.

The Friendlies and the Plantains.

The Chin militia gave one of these hard bargainers a good lesson once. A

Chin had prowled round the camp with a basket of plantains for sale. But, as his prices were high, he had found no purchasers; so he strolled into the camp of the friendlies, hoping to do business with his own countrymen, no doubt. These strapping, sturdy, young fellows were a devil-may-care set of semi-savages, and always ready for a lark. Before the Chin with his basket of plantains could say Jack Robinson, or whatever the equivalent is in Chin, the friendlies sprang on him and emptied his basket in no time. Then they tossed the bewildered man about from one to the other, and soon nothing was left of the few rags in which he had been clothed. An old patriarchal Chin now came up and, tapping the man on the shoulder, fixed him with his stern eye and spoke to him thus:— "O foolish child of the hills! you know the character of your fel- low tribes- men. If they want a thing, they take it, by foul means if they can't get it by fair! It was fool- ish of you to come here to *sell* your plan- tains. Don't

GARHWALI ESCORT BRINGING IN CHIN PRISONERS.

do it again! But show me the man who took your plantains, and I'll see if I can restore them to you." He said this with a scowl at the shivering man, while with one eye he winked round on the grinning friendlies as much as to say, "Doesn't he wish he may get them!" The Chin, however, thought he had had enough of this game and so waited to hear no more, but, gathering up the shreds of his rags, slunk off into the jungle. Some of us were spectators of this scene from a distance, and it was fully as good as a bit from a Christmas pantomime.

The Chins Despatch their Enemies Promptly.

We never heard any stories showing that the Chins treated their enemies cruelly. Their method of treating an enemy was at all events expeditious. They waited for him behind a tree and shot him, or, if he was captured, his throat was cut. But they have never resorted to torture and cruelty.

The Blood-Feud.

The blood-feud is the Chin's universal method of avenging murder. The opposing factions go on shooting one another, whenever they get the chance, and thus the feuds become interminable. When a Chin slays his enemy, the event, as usual, is celebrated with feasting and drinking, and a raid-trophy is erected. It is a proud and happy moment for a Chin when he kills an hereditary foe; he boasts of the events, and is considered quite a hero in his own village. The following incident illustrates this. While the column was passing through a village, the Political Officer noticed a brand new raid-trophy and asked who had put it up. Everybody replied that so and so was the hero. And the hero himself, a relative of the Chief's, came forward and proudly declared that he had had the honour of putting up the trophy, and that he was the fortunate individual who had been privileged to wipe the blood-stain from off his house and family. Then he related how the man he had slain had been an hereditary enemy of his, and how he had gone down to his village, waylaid, and shot him, and so his conscience was now free; and he looked round triumphantly, believing his recital had produced a deep impression on the crowd. The villages of both factions were now under our control, and the authorities were desirous that these blood-feuds should be put an end to. A beginning had to be made some time or other, although it might appear hard on the first few cases. The man was, therefore,

BURNING OF TUNZAN, WHERE STEWART'S HEAD WAS FOUND.

arrested, and, much to his astonishment, was informed that such actions could no longer be tolerated ; that we considered it murder, and would punish the culprits accordingly. However, to stamp out effectually the blood-feud, which has been a law unto the Chins ever since they can remember, will be a matter of time. This man was subsequently tried and condemned to a period of imprisonment in Burma.

Their Graves.

The Chins bury their dead in their own yards. At Falam we found the graves in the yards covered over with little thatched sheds, and in the Chiefs' houses there were solid stone-and-cement places which looked like vaults, in which the departed Chiefs slept their long sleep. In no other village had we come across such tombs. People who die violent deaths are buried outside the village. In such places they erect rudely carved posts, surmounted by skulls of animals, and with slabs of stone below. These are usually at the entrances of villages and near shady trees, and they also serve as resting-places, where the traveller can sit down in the shade and rest. When you come across these posts, you can always tell a village is in the neighbourhood.

JAHOOTA, THE PRESENT KLUNG-KLUNG CHIEF, AND HIS RELATIVES.

The manner of arranging these posts varies with each tribe, as a reference to the photographs will show. They are most plentiful in the southern Boungshay country. Sometimes, at the entrances of villages, we came across recent graves of men killed during raids. Such graves were surrounded by a wooden palisade, to

FORT WHITE.
Thacker, Spink & Co., Calcutta

which were attached the skulls of animals killed by the deceased. In the centre of the enclosure is a post, on which are hung the deceased's rain-coat, pipe, water gourd and other articles he used during his lifetime. At the foot of the post are vessels of water and food, so that, should the departed spirit return hungry and thirsty, he could eat and drink, and then go away satisfied and not haunt the village. From one of these posts we found suspended a human scalp and a pair of ears, the property of an enemy of the deceased, whom he had slain before he met with his own end.

The Tipsy Chief.

ON THE LOOK-OUT FOR THE OTHER COLUMN.

On one occasion the column arrived before a large village, from which several shots suddenly rang out. "Halloa! Is the village going to fight?" was the thought that occurred to each of us. But we soon found there was a big feast on —either a funeral or a marriage—and all the villagers were drunk! Presently the old Chief appeared with his retinue, all far gone. The Chief was just able to keep on his pins, but to show his joy at our arrival he broke into a fantastic dance, a roll down the hill now and again not in the least cooling his ardour. Finally he lifted up his voice and welcomed us to his village, as with red, bleary eyes and dripping mouth he grinned into each of our faces; and finally, much to the amusement of the whole column, he wound up by embracing the Commanding Officer and then in turn the others, all of whom he stroked like so many cats. His attentions at last became so overpowering that we had to get the old man removed from camp.

"The Sage of Shurkwa."

Another Chin toper also came to be well known during the Boungshay expeditions. We knew him as old "Tetapata" or "the Sage of Shurkwa." In 1891, when a column from Haka began to shell Shurkwa from the opposite hill (as the village had been defiant and refused to submit) the Shurkwa people thought better of it and sent down a deputation of two men to offer their submission. One of these two men was the old Sage referred to above. As the shells went shrieking across the valley, the column suddenly saw two Chins rushing down the *khud* at a headlong pace from the village, each staggering under the load of a miscellaneous collection of fowls, plan-tains, sugar-cane, and gourds of *Yu*. Before any orders could be given, some of the sepoys fired a volley or two at the two figures, but luckily the shooting was not straight and no damage was done. However, this only served to quicken the speed at which the two heavily laden Chins came bounding down the hill, clearing ditches and other obstacles like antelopes. It was quite a ludicrous sight. They soon came up the hill on which the column was halted and made known their mission. Peace was accordingly concluded and ratified in the usual Chin manner, the Sage taking the principal part on behalf of the Shurkwas. During the ceremony the formula rattled off by the old Sage consisted chiefly of the sounds "*Te-ta-pa-ta*," repeated in rapid succession. From this incident he received his *sobriquet*. Immediately after the ceremony the old man, always with an eye to business, rushed off and commenced to pick up all the empty bulli-beef tins and other rubbish he found lying about, with which he

TASHON COLUMN ENCAMPED NEAR SOURCES OF THE BOINU.

THE C. O. AND HIS STAFF-OFFICER INTERVIEWING A CHIN CHIEF, "OLD TETAPATA."
Thacker, Spink & Co., Calcutta.

returned in triumph to the village. He was a dirty old man of about fifty winters, with a scraggy gray beard and gray hair and a 'cute-looking face with overhanging brows, from beneath which looked out a pair of small sharp eyes, that gave you the impression that they were always on the look-out for the main chance. From the angles of his mouth tobacco-juice always kept oozing in drops and stained his grizzly old beard. The old boy we soon discovered had a great fondness for *Yu* and rum, when he could get any. Wherever there was a *Yu* jar or gourd lying about, there you would be sure to find old "Tetapata" also. His eyes were usually pink in the morning, and assuredly, had the colour of his skin permitted it, a boiled lobster would have been pale by the side of his nose! He attached himself to the friendlies with the column, and came out with us on several "dours." This apparently he did on the chance of getting free and unlimited drinks at all the villages. He was a proficient in sucking the stuff out of the jars, by which he sat longer than anyone else, and the twinkle of satisfaction in his little eyes as the liquid trickled down his throat was a sight worth seeing. He often came and sat by our fire and tried to make himself agreeable, keeping one eye all the while on the rum-bottle. There was no resisting this mute appeal, and the satisfaction with which he smacked his lips and grunted out, "*Atah! Atah!*" (good! very good!) was worth the price of the tot given him. Whenever or wherever you met the old man, climbing a hill, or fording a river, or resting by the wayside, he always produced an orange from somewhere beneath his capacious, but dirty, robes, and presented it to you: it was usually sour! He

EVENING AT A POST ON THE CHIN HILLS.

was a good forager too, and sometimes did a little trade with us. He looted fowls from the villages on the way and sold them to us. When times were hard, he strode about the camp in a stately sort of way selling oranges and things. One day he astonished us all by shaving off his beard, and this gave him quite a juvenile appearance. He was a domesticated old man too, for he often came into camp with his child slung on his shoulders. He was useful in obtaining Chin coolies and in other ways. I much regret to record that subsequently, in the little disturbance that occurred at Shurkwa about coolies, old "Tetapata," in trying to smooth matters between the two parties,

"FORT GUNNING," THE POST IN THE HOUNGSHAY COUNTRY NEAR LOTAW.

COLUMN HALTED PREVIOUS TO FINAL ADVANCE ON FALAM, THE TASHON CAPITAL.

was shot dead. Poor old Chin! He wasn't a bad savage at heart, and we were all sorry to hear of his untimely end.

The Chin who kept his mouth open.

During the shelling of a village one friendly old Chief did not like the noise made by the guns and seemed half inclined to run away. Some one told him that, if he kept his mouth wide open and stuck his fingers into his ears, he would suffer no injury. Whereupon the old man promptly opened his mouth as wide as it would go, and much to everyone's amusement sat patiently in that attitude till the firing ceased!

LEARNING THE CHIN LANGUAGE.

How we fed.

Our feeding arrangements were not the same in all the columns. In some we had one big mess, while in others there were several small ones. Both methods worked equally well, though we got more fun out of the small messes. Each mess was known by a number. Thus, when dinner was ready, you would hear such shouts as:—"Roll up, No. 1, for dinner!" or "Hurry up, No. 2!" or "Pull yourselves together, No. 3!"

THE HOUSES WE LIVE IN AT A CHIN POST.

Always late!" And then each mess sat round its own fire and discussed its own dinner. Our fires were adjacent to one another, so that, as the meal went on, we were able to talk across to each other and criticise each other's *menus* for the day, something after this fashion :—"We have got an excellent stew to-day. What have you got, No. 1?" "Oh! our omelette is simply beautiful. We have never tasted a better in all our lives before!" would reply No. 1. "But we have such a beauty of a custard. Your *chef* could not make one like it, if he tried all his life!" would chime in No. 3 mess.

"Pooh!" would put in No. 4. "We have a roast fowl here, that will beat anything you could produce." And so amidst jesting and pleasant chatter the dinner-hour would pass away merrily. Sometimes one mess invited another across to dinner; but the invitation stated that you had to bring your own food and drink when you came! Then, when you called on the other messes, say, to leave your card, you were asked to have a peg, but you had to provide it yourself!

THE HAKA POST.

We are a Happy Family.

Throughout the whole period we were a happy family. Each one contributed, as far as in him lay, to the general enjoyment. And the happy spirit and thorough fellow-feeling that always prevailed caused all difficulties to vanish.

The Story of the Free Drink.

Before concluding these camp reminiscences, we cannot refrain from quoting a story of how a thirsty young officer got an extra free drink. We had all come

A CONSULTATION: MR. CAREY, MR. MACNABB, MAJOR HOWLETT, AND CAPT. EVATT.
Thacker, Spink & Co. Calcutta.

into camp after a long weary march. A Tommy marched in looking very worn and fagged out. The thirsty officer thereupon poured out a stiff peg of rum from the mess bottle and said he would give it to the tired soldier. He went to the man and offered him the rum; but he said, "Much obliged, sir, but I am a teetotaller." "Oh! I am very sorry; I did not know that," said the thirsty one, and he promptly drank off the peg himself; and that is how he got an extra drink all for nothing. But it brought him in for a good deal of chaff and banter.

CHINS BRINGING ON THE MAILS.

Work Successfully Done.

In spite of difficulties, many and varied, which need not be set down here, the Expeditions were, one and all, most successfully accomplished, and that without resort to bloodshed. And does not Milton tell us, "Peace hath her victories no less renown'd than war?"

Though we fought no battles, yet the toiling and moiling over that interminable jumble of hills, which tried the endurance of the troops to the utmost, represented a sum total of very hard work done. And the troops richly earned the high encomiums bestowed on them by the military authorities.

The Work Done.

The whole of these hills has now been traversed from end to end, and the submission of all the tribes obtained, though, so long as they have their fire-arms, there is the chance of disturbances occurring at any time—as was the case recently at Shurkwa. Many Burmese captives were released, especially in the north by Mr. Carey. Raiding into Burma has now ceased. The Klung-Klung tribes, who were concerned in the attack on our troops last year, were duly punished by heavy fines of guns and, where they refused to pay, by the burning of a house for every gun not paid. The village where Lieut. Stewart's head was found was also punished, the headmen's houses being burnt and the village heavily fined in guns, while the murder-trophies were all de- stroyed. The Klung-Klung ex-Chief Lalway, remains a fugitive in the hills, and a relation of his, well known as "Jahoota," reigns in his stead as Chief of the Klung-Klung tribes. In the north the Kanhow column found a very good trade-route direct into Manipur. The Tashon column had the honour of discovering the sources of the Boinu or Kolodyne river, in longitude 90° 32' and latitude 22° 51', on the 29th of March, 1892, in a morass to the west of the great Ramklao range.

CHIN HILLS AND VILLAGE.

Temporary Posts.

After the various expeditions were over, temporary posts were established in different parts of the hills, from which small parties from time to time went out and visited vill- ages, that the expeditions had not been able to visit. And thus our troops were en évidence in every direct- ion. When the rains set in, these posts were all with- drawn. A new per- manent post was established at Falam, the Tashon capital.

SENDING OUT RATIONS FOR A COLUMN.

Conclusion of Operations.

With the breaking-up of the columns, the troops who came up temporarily for the operations joyfully return to Burma, hoping never to see the Chin Hills again. The rest settle down in their posts to hibernate till the next open season, when they will have to take their share again in any work that may have to be done. For during the rains nothing can be accomplished.

THE POLITICAL COURT AT HAKA.

There are now three main posts in these hills. These are Haka in the south, Fort White in the north, and Falam in the centre. These posts are garrisoned respectively by the 2nd Burma Battalion, the 1st Burma Rifles, and the 39th Gurhwal Rifles.

The Present Situation.

Such is the situation in the Chin Hills at the present moment. A Chin-Lushai Conference recently met at Calcutta to decide on the future policy to be pursued in reference to these hills. The Government of India has now published the result, which is, that Lushai-land, converted into one charge, is to be handed over to Assam, while the Chin Hills, also probably made into one charge, will continue to be administered by Burma.

IN THE STOCKS.

THE END

MEETING OF THE CHIEFS: THE C.O.'S AND THE POLITICAL OFFICERS OF THE TASHON AND NWENGAL COLUMNS ARRANGING THEIR PLAN OF CAMPAIGN.

No. 61. *February,* 1894.

A Select Catalogue of Works,
Chiefly Illustrated, published by W THACKER & CO., 87 Newgate Street, London, and THACKER SPINK & CO., Calcutta.

BANIAN TREE.

TO BE OBTAINED ALSO OF

THACKER & CO., Limited, Bombay.

W. THACKER & CO, 87 *NEWGATE STREET, LONDON.*

THE IMAGE OF WAR: Service on the Chin Hills. By Surgeon-Captain A. G. E. Newland.

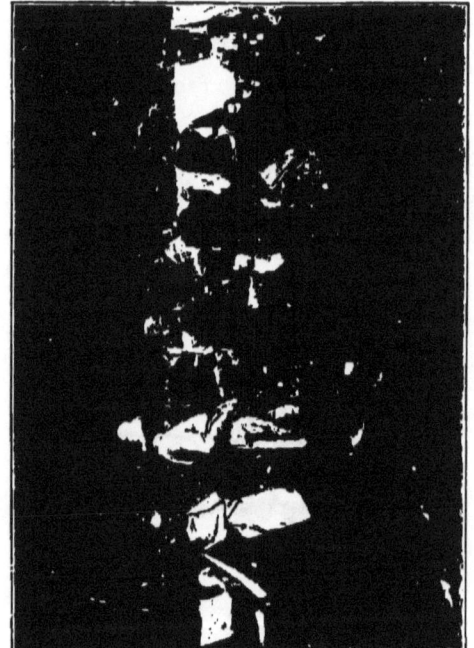

194 Illustrations from Instantaneous Photographs. Demy 4to. £1 11s. 6d.

W. THACKER & CO., 87 NEWGATE STREET, LONDON.

THACKER, SPINK & CO., CALCUTTA.

Messrs. THACKER, SPINK & CO. will shortly publish a work unique in its character and extremely beautiful in its form, entitled,

THE IMAGE OF WAR; or, Service on the Chin Hills.

By SURGEON-CAPTAIN A. G. E. NEWLAND.

With an Introductory Historical Note by J. D. MACNABB, Esq., *Political Officer, South Chin Hills. Demy 4to.*

POLITICAL OFFICER RECEIVING SUBMISSION OF TASHON CHIEFS.

It is illustrated by 34 full-page Collotypes of Instantaneous Photographs, and 160 interspersed in the reading. No work has yet appeared, in Europe or America, of this beautiful character. The price to subscribers is Rs. 25, but as only a small edition is printed, Messrs Thacker, Spink & Co. hold themselves at liberty to raise the price upon publication to Rs. 30. From its nature the book cannot be reprinted, and subscribers will possess a work of extreme beauty, interest and rarity.

W. THACKER & CO., 87 NEWGATE STREET, LONDON.

THACKER, SPINK & CO., CALCUTTA.

A NATURALIST ON THE PROWL.

PYTHON CRUSHING MONKEY. (FROM INSTANTANEOUS PHOTOGRAPH.)

By EHA, Author of "Tribes on my Frontier," etc.

W. THACKER & CO., 87 NEWGATE STREET, LONDON.

THACKER, SPINK & CO, CALCUTTA.

In the Press, a new work by that popular writer, EHA, Author of "THE TRIBES ON MY FRONTIER," and "BEHIND THE BUNGALOW," called

A NATURALIST ON THE PROWL.

Profusely Illustrated by Drawings by Mr. R. A. STERNDALE, F.R.G.S., F.Z.S. Author of "Mammalia of India," "Denizens of the Jungle," "Seonee," etc., who has studied and sketched animals of all kinds in their habitat and at work.

JACKAL ON THE PROWL.

EHA cannot be dull, and the book will not only be uniform with the former popular works, but fully equal in interest and life.

W. THACKER & CO., 87 NEWGATE STREET, LONDON.

Fifth Edition. In Imperial 16mo, uniform with "Lays of Ind," "Riding," "Hindu Mythology," etc. 8s. 6d.

THE TRIBES ON MY FRONTIER:
An Indian Naturalist's Foreign Policy.
By EHA.
WITH FIFTY ILLUSTRATIONS BY F. C. MACRAE.

N this remarkably clever work there are most graphically and humorously described the surroundings of a Mofussil bungalow. The twenty chapters embrace a year's experiences, and provide endless sources of amusement and suggestion. The numerous able illustrations add very greatly to the interest of the volume, which will find a place on every table.

THE CHAPTERS ARE—

I.—A Durbar.
II.—The Rats.
III.—The Mosquitos.
IV.—The Lizards.
V.—The Ants.
VI.—The Crows.
VII.—The Bats.
VIII.—Bees, Wasps, et hoc genus omne.
IX.—The Spiders.
X.—The Butterfly: Hunting Him.
XI.—The Butterfly: Contemplating Him.
XII.—The Frogs.
XIII.—The Bugs.
XIV.—The Birds of the Garden.
XV.—The Birds at the Mango Tope.
XVI.—The Birds at the Tank.
XVII.—The Poultry Yard.
XVIII.—The White Ants.
XIX.—The Hypodermatikosyringophoroi.
XX.—Etcetera.

W. THACKER & CO., 87 NEWGATE STREET, LONDON.

THACKER, SPINK & CO., CALCUTTA.

THE TRIBES ON MY FRONTIER.

Fifth Edition. 8s. 6d.

"It is a very clever record of a year's observations round the bungalow in 'Dustypore.' . . . . It is by no means a mere travesty. . . . . The writer is always amusing, and never dull."—*Field.*

"The book is cleverly illustrated by Mr. F. C. Macrae. We have only to thank our Anglo-Indian naturalist for the delightful book which he has sent home to his countrymen in Britain. May he live to give us another such."—*Chambers's Journal.*

"A most charming series of sprightly and entertaining essays on what may be termed the fauna of the Indian bungalow. . . . . We have no doubt that this amusing book will find its way into every Anglo-Indian's library."—*Allen's Indian Mail.*

"This is a delightful book, irresistibly funny in description and illustration, but full of genuine science too. . . . . There is not a dull or uninstructive page in the whole book."—*Knowledge.*

"It is a pleasantly written book about the insects and other torments of India which make Anglo-Indian life unpleasant, and which can be read with pleasure even by those beyond the reach of the tormenting things Eha describes."—*Graphic.*

"The volume is full of accurate and unfamiliar observation."
—*Saturday Review.*

W. THACKER & CO., 87 NEWGATE STREET, LONDON.

Fourth Edition, Imperial 16mo. 6s.

BEHIND THE BUNGALOW.

BY EHA,
AUTHOR OF "TRIBES ON MY FRONTIER."

WITH FIFTY-THREE CLEVER SKETCHES
By the Illustrator of "The Tribes."

As "The Tribes on my Frontier" graphically and humorously described the Animal Surroundings of an Indian Bungalow, the present work describes with much pleasantry the Human Officials thereof, with their peculiarities, idiosyncrasies, and, to the European, strange methods of duty. Each chapter contains Character Sketches by the Illustrator of "The Tribes," and the work is a "Natural History" of the Native Tribes who in India render us service.

W. THACKER & CO., 87 NEWGATE STREET, LONDON.

THACKER, SPINK & CO., CALCUTTA.

"There is plenty of fun in 'Behind the Bungalow,' and more than fun for those with eyes to see. These sketches may have an educational purpose beyond that of mere amusement; they show through all their fun a keen observation of native character and a just appreciation of it."
—*The World.*

BEHIND THE BUNGALOW.
By the Author of "TRIBES ON MY FRONTIER."
AND ILLUSTRATED BY THE SAME ARTIST.

"'The Tribes On My Frontier' was very good : 'Behind the Bungalow' is even better. Anglo-Indians will see how truthful are these sketches. People who know nothing about India will delight in the clever drawings and the truly humorous descriptions; and, their appetite for fun being gratified, they will not fail to note the undercurrent of sympathy."
—*The Graphic.*

"The native members of an Anglo-Indian household are hit off with great fidelity and humour."—*The Queen.*

W. THACKER & CO., 87 NEWGATE STREET, LONDON.

THACKER, SPINK & CO., CALCUTTA.

LAYS OF IND. By ALIPH CHEEM.
COMIC, SATIRICAL, AND DESCRIPTIVE

Poems Illustrative of Anglo-Indian Life.

ILLUSTRATED BY THE AUTHOR, LIONEL INGLIS, R. A. STERNDALE, AND OTHERS.

Ninth Edition. Cloth, gilt. 10s. 6d.

"This is a remarkably bright little book. 'Aliph Cheem,' supposed to be the *nom de plume* of an officer in the 18th Hussars, is, after his fashion, an Indian Bon Gaultier. In a few of the poems the jokes, turning on local names and customs, are somewhat esoteric; but, taken throughout, the verses are characterized by high animal spirits, great cleverness, and most excellent fooling."—*The World.*

"One can readily imagine the merriment created round the camp fire by the recitation of 'The Two Thumpers,' which is irresistibly droll. . . . The edition before us is enlarged, and contains illustrations by the author, in addition to which it is beautifully printed and handsomely got up, all which recommendations are sure to make the name of Aliph Cheem more popular in India than ever."—*Liverpool Mercury.*

"Satire of the most amusing and inoffensive kind, humour the most genuine, and pathos the most touching pervade these 'Lays of Ind.' . . . From Indian friends we have heard of the popularity these 'Lays' have obtained in the land where they were written, and we predict for them a popularity equally great at home."—*Monthly Homœopathic Review.*

W. THACKER & CO., 87 NEWGATE STREET, LONDON.

THACKER, SPINK & CO., CALCUTTA.

Reviews of "Lays of Ind."

"The 'Lays' are not only Anglo-Indian in origin, but out-and-out Anglo-Indian in subject and colour. To one who knows something of life at an Indian 'station' they will be especially amusing. Their exuberant fun at the same time may well attract the attention of the ill-defined individual known as 'the general reader.'"—*Scotsman.*

"To many Anglo-Indians the lively verses of 'Aliph Cheem' must be very well known, while to those who have not yet become acquainted with them we can only say read them on the first opportunity. To those not familiar with Indian life they may be specially commended for the picture which they give of many of its lighter incidents and conditions, and of several of its ordinary personages."—*Bath Chronicle.*

Seventh Edition. In square 32mo. 5s.

DEPARTMENTAL DITTIES AND OTHER VERSES,

Humorous and Character Poems of Anglo-Indian Life.

BY RUDYARD KIPLING.

"They reflect with light gaiety the thoughts and feelings of actual men and women, and are true as well as clever. . . . Mr. Kipling achieves the feat of making Anglo-Indian society flirt and intrigue visibly before our eyes. . . . His book gives hope of a new literary star of no mean magnitude rising in the East."
—SIR W. W. HUNTER, *in The Academy.*

"As for that terrible, scathing piece, 'The Story of Uriah,' we know of nothing with which to compare it, and one cannot help the wretched feeling that it is true. . . . 'In Spring Time' is the most pathetic lament of an exile we know in modern poetry."—*Graphic.*

RHYMING LEGENDS OF IND.

By H. K. GRACEY, B.A., C.S.   *Crown 8vo, 6s.*

"A series of lively Stories in Verse."—*Times.*

"Are not only amusing, but are lively descriptions of scenery and customs in Indian Life. . . . Cleverly and humorously told."—*Weekly Times.*

W. THACKER & CO., 87 NEWGATE STREET, LONDON.

THACKER, SPINK & CO., CALCUTTA.

Crown 8vo. 6s.

COW KEEPING IN INDIA.
A Simple and Practical Book on

Their Care and Treatment, their various Breeds,
AND
THE MEANS OF RENDERING THEM PROFITABLE.

BY ISA TWEED.

CROWN 8vo.
With Thirty-Nine Illustrations, including the various Breeds of Cattle, drawn from Photographs by
R. A. STERNDALE.

W. THACKER & CO., 87 NEWGATE STREET, LONDON.

NEARLY READY.

DOGS FOR HOT CLIMATES.

BY VERO SHAW.
Author of Cassell's "Book of the Dog." Late Kennel Editor of the "Field."

AND

CAPTAIN M. H. HAYES, F.R.C.V.S.
Author of "Veterinary Notes," etc.

The book will be illustrated by typical animals of each breed treated of, chiefly from Photographs of Prize Winners, and will be essential to all lovers of the Dog in Hot Climates. It will be uniform with "Cow Keeping in India," "Poultry Keeping in India," etc.

W. THACKER & CO., 87 NEWGATE STREET, LONDON.

THACKER, SPINK & CO., CALCUTTA.

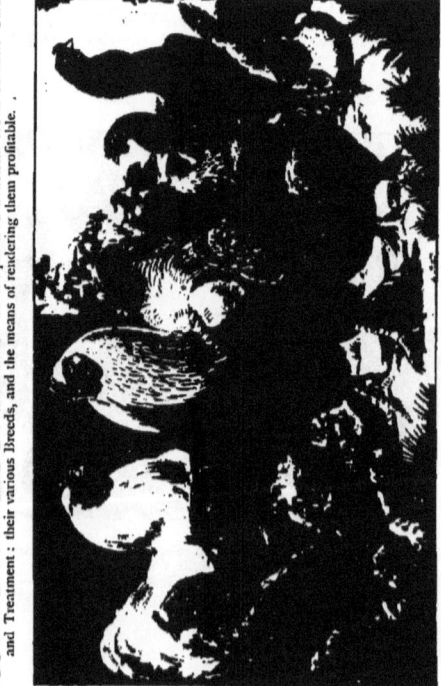

POULTRY KEEPING IN INDIA. In Crown 8vo. Illustrated. A Simple and Practical Book on their Care and Treatment: their various Breeds, and the means of rendering them profitable. By ISA TWEED, Author of "Cow Keeping in India."

W. THACKER & CO., 87 NEWGATE STREET, LONDON.

The Second Edition, Revised, and with additional Illustrations by the Author.
Post 8vo. 8s. 6d.

SEONEE:
OR,
CAMP LIFE ON THE SATPURA RANGE.
A Tale of Indian Adventure.

By R. A. STERNDALE,
AUTHOR OF "MAMMALIA OF INDIA," "DENIZENS OF THE JUNGLE."

Illustrated by the Author.

With an Appendix containing a brief Topographical and Historical account of the District of Seonee in the Central Provinces of India.

W. THACKER & CO., 87 NEWGATE STREET, LONDON.

THACKER, SPINK & CO., CALCUTTA.

In Imperial 16mo. Uniform with "Riding," "Riding for Ladies," "Hindu Mythology." 12s. 6d.

A NATURAL HISTORY
OF THE
MAMMALIA OF INDIA,
BURMAH AND CEYLON.
BY R. A. STERNDALE, F.R.G.S., F.Z.S., ETC.,
AUTHOR OF "SEONEE," "THE DENIZENS OF THE JUNGLE," "THE AFGHAN KNIFE," ETC.

WITH 170 ILLUSTRATIONS BY THE AUTHOR AND OTHERS.

The geographical limits of the present work have been extended to all territories likely to be reached by the sportsman from India. It is copiously illustrated, not only by the author himself, but by careful selections made by him from the works of well-known artists.

"It is the very model of what a popular natural history should be."—*Knowledge.*
"An amusing work with good illustrations."—*Nature.*
"Full of accurate observation, brightly told."—*Saturday Review.*
"The results of a close and sympathetic observation."—*Athenæum.*
"It has the brevity which is the soul of wit, and a delicacy of allusion which charms the literary critic."—*Academy.*
"The notices of each animal are, as a rule, short, though on some of the larger mammals—the lion, tiger, pard, boar, etc.,—ample and interesting details are given, including occasional anecdotes of adventure. The book will, no doubt, be specially useful to the sportsman, and, indeed, has been extended so as to include all territories likely to be reached by the sportsman from India. Those who desire to obtain some general information, popularly conveyed, on the subject with which the book deals, will, we believe, find it useful."—*The Times.*
"Has contrived to hit a happy mean between the stiff scientific treatise and the bosh of what may be called anecdotal zoology."—*The Daily News.*

W. THACKER & CO., 87 NEWGATE STREET, LONDON.

THACKER, SPINK & CO., CALCUTTA.

Foolscap 8vo, with 8 Maps. *Rs.* 3-8.

THE SPORTSMAN'S MANUAL

IN QUEST OF GAME

IN KULLU, LAHOUL AND LADAK, TO THE TSO MORARI LAKES.

WITH NOTES ON SHOOTING IN SPITI, BARA BAGAHAL, CHAMBA AND KASHMIR;
AND A DETAILED DESCRIPTION OF SPORT IN MORE THAN 130 NALAS.

BY

LIEUT.-COL. R. H. TYACKE.

LATE H.M.'s 98TH AND 34TH REGIMENTS.

Oblong Imperial 4to. 16s.

DENIZENS OF THE JUNGLES:

A Series of Sketches of Wild Animals,

ILLUSTRATING THEIR FORMS AND NATURAL ATTITUDES. WITH LETTERPRESS
DESCRIPTION OF EACH PLATE.

By R. A. STERNDALE, F.R.G.S., F.Z.S.,

AUTHOR OF "NATURAL HISTORY OF THE MAMMALIA OF INDIA," "SEONEE," ETC.

1. Denizens of the Jungles.—*Aborigines—Deer—Monkeys.*
2. On the Watch.—*Tiger.*
3. Not so fast Asleep as he Looks.—*Panther—Monkeys.*
4. Waiting for Father.—*Black Bears of the Plains.*
5. Rival Monarchs. — *Tiger and Elephant.*
6. Hors de Combat.—*Indian Wild Boar and Tiger.*
7. A Race for Life. — *Blue Bull and Wild Dogs.*
8. Meaning Mischief.—*The Gaur—Indian Bison.*
9. More than His Match.—*Buffalo and Rhinoceros.*
10. A Critical Moment. — *Spotted Deer and Leopard.*
11. Hard hit—*The Sambur.*
12. Mountain Monarchs. — *Marco Polo's Sheep.*

"The plates are admirably executed by photo-lithography from the author's originals, every line and touch being faithfully preserved. It is a volume which will be eagerly studied on many a table. Many an amusing and exciting anecdote add to the general interest of the work."—*Broad Arrow.*

"The Volume is well got up and the drawings are spirited and natural."—*Illustrated London News.*

W. THACKER & CO., 87 NEWGATE STREET, LONDON.

THACKER, SPINK & CO., CALCUTTA.

GAME, SHORE,
AND
WATER BIRDS
OF INDIA.
BY
COL. A. LE MESSURIER,
R.E.

121 ILLUSTRATIONS.

8vo, 15s.

*A VADE ME-
CUM FOR THE
SPORTSMAN,
EMBRACING ALL THE
BIRDS AT ALL LIKELY TO
BE MET WITH IN A
SHOOTING EXCURSION.*

"Compact in form, excellent in method and arrangement, and, as far as we have been able to test it, rigidly accurate."—*Knowledge.*

"Will be a source of great delight, as every ornithological detail is given, in conjunction with the most artistic and exquisite drawings."—*Home News.*

W. THACKER & CO., 87 NEWGATE STREET, LONDON.

THACKER, SPINK & CO., CALCUTTA.

"Splendidly Illustrated Record of Sport."—*Graphic.*

Third Edition. Enlarged. Demy 4to. 36 Plates and Map. £2 2s.

LARGE GAME SHOOTING
IN THIBET, THE HIMALAYAS, NORTHERN & CENTRAL INDIA.
By Brig.-General ALEX. A. A. KINLOCH.

Reduced size.

"Colonel Kinloch, who has killed most kinds of Indian game, small and great, relates incidents of his varied sporting experiences in chapters, which are each descriptive of a different animal. The photo-gravures of the heads of many of the animals, from the grand gaur, popularly miscalled the bison, downwards, are extremely clever and spirited."—*Times.*

W. THACKER & CO., 87 NEWGATE STREET, LONDON.

New Edition, Demy 8vo, with all Original Illustrations. Rs. 7-8.

THE HIGHLANDS OF CENTRAL INDIA.
NOTES ON THEIR
Forests and Wild Tribes, Natural History and Sport.

By CAPT. J. FORSYTH, BENGAL STAFF CORPS.
WITH
ILLUSTRATIONS BY R. A. STERNDALE, F.Z.S., F.R.G.S.

In Demy folio, Thirty-nine Plates, Natural Size. 25s.

ILLUSTRATIONS OF THE
GRASSES OF THE SOUTHERN PUNJAB.
BEING

Photo-Lithographs of some of the Grasses found at Hissar, with Descriptive Letterpress.

By WILLIAM COLDSTREAM, B.A., B.C.S.

W. THACKER & CO., 87 NEWGATE STREET, LONDON.

Fourth Edition, Crown 8vo, Buckram. 12s. 6d.

VETERINARY NOTES FOR HORSE-OWNERS.

An Illustrated Manual of Horse Medicine and Surgery, written in Simple Language.

By CAPT. M. H. HAYES, F.R.C.V.S.

"Captain Hayes' work is a valuable addition to our stable literature; and the illustrations, tolerably numerous, are excellent beyond the reach of criticism."—*Saturday Review.*

"The description of symptoms and proper methods of treatment in sickness render the book a necessary guide for horseowners, especially those who are far removed from immediate professional assistance."—*The Times.*

"Of the many popular veterinary books which have come under our notice, this is certainly one of the most scientific and reliable. If some painstaking student would give us works of equal merit to this on the diseases of the other domestic animals, we should possess a very complete veterinary library in a very small compass."—*Field.*

"Simplicity is one of the most commendable features in the book. What Captain Hayes has to say he says in plain terms, and the book is a very useful one for everybody who is concerned with horses."—*Illustrated Sporting and Dramatic News.*

"The usefulness of the manual is testified to by its popularity, and each edition has given evidence of increasing care on the part of the author to render it more complete and trustworthy as a book of reference for amateurs."—*The Lancet.*

"A volume replete with most interesting information, couched in the simplest terms possible."—*The County Gentleman.*

"The book leaves nothing to be desired on the score of lucidity and comprehensiveness."—*Veterinary Journal.*

W. THACKER & CO., 87 *NEWGATE STREET, LONDON.*

THACKER, SPINK & CO., CALCUTTA.

Square 8vo, 10s. 6d.

THE HORSEWOMAN.
A PRACTICAL GUIDE TO SIDE-SADDLE RIDING.
BY MRS. HAYES. EDITED BY CAPTAIN M. H. HAYES.

With 4 Collotypes from Instantaneous Photographs, and 48 Drawings after Photographs, by J. H. OSWALD BROWN.

PRESS NOTICES.

The Times.—"A large amount of sound, practical instruction, very judiciously and pleasantly imparted."

The Field.—"This is the first occasion on which a practical horseman and a practical horsewoman have collaborated in bringing out a book on riding for ladies. The result is in every way satisfactory, and, no matter how well a lady

W. THACKER & CO., 87 NEWGATE STREET, LONDON.

THACKER, SPINK & CO., CALCUTTA.

THE HORSEWOMAN.

PRESS NOTICES.—(*Continued.*)

may ride, she will gain much valuable information from a perusal of 'The Horsewoman.' The book is happily free from self-laudatory passages."

The Athenæum.—"We have seldom come across a brighter book than 'The Horsewoman.'

The Queen.—"A most useful and practical book on side-saddle riding, which may be read with real interest by all lady riders."

Freeman's Journal (Dublin).—"Mrs. Hayes is perhaps the best authority in these countries on everything connected with horsemanship for ladies."

Scotsman (Edinburgh).—"The work is the outcome of experiences, aptitudes, and opportunities wholly exceptional."

Le Sport (Paris).—"J'ai lu ou parcouru bien des traités d'équitation usuelle ou savante; jamais encore je n'avais trouvé un exposé aussi clair, aussi simple, aussi vécu que celui où Mme. Hayes résume les principes dont une pratique assidue lui a permis d'apprécier la valeur. Ce très remarquable manuel d'équitation féminine est bien, comme la desire son auteur, à la portée de tous et il est à souhaiter qu'il trouvé en France l'accueil et le succès qu'il à rencontrés dès sa publication auprès des horsewomen anglaises."

Saturday Review.—"With a very strong recommendation of this book as far and away the best guide to side-saddle riding that we have seen."

The Queen.—"It is a real pleasure to see a lady ride as Mrs. Hayes does; she combines in an unusual degree an absolutely firm, strong seat with a pretty and graceful one."

Land and Water.—"A more thorough horsewoman than Mrs. Hayes probably does not exist."

Hearth and Home.—"The Duke of Cambridge personally complimented her on her seat and hands."

Indian Planters' Gazette (Calcutta).—"The victory [in jumping competition] was well earned. Mrs. Hayes treated the large crowd to an exhibition of horsemanship, the like of which has seldom, if ever, been witnessed in Calcutta. The merit of the performance is enhanced by the fact that she had never ridden the mare before that day."

The Mining Argus (Johannesburg, Transvaal).—"Mrs. Hayes is undoubtedly one of the pluckiest and most accomplished horsewomen we have ever seen."

North China Daily News (Shanghai).—"This accomplished horsewoman practically illustrated, for the benefit of the ladies present, what she wrote in our columns about riding without reins, even over stiff jumps, on a mount only broken for a lady ten minutes before."

W. THACKER & CO., 87 NEWGATE STREET, LONDON.

THACKER, SPINK & CO., CALCUTTA.

Third Edition, Imperial 16mo. 10s. 6d.

RIDING:
ON THE FLAT AND ACROSS COUNTRY.
A Guide to Practical Horsemanship.
By Captain M. H. HAYES, F.R.C.V.S.

The Times.—"Captain Hayes' hints and instructions are useful aids, even to experienced riders, while for those less accustomed to the saddle, his instructions are simply invaluable."

The Standard.—"Captain Hayes is not only a master of his subject, but he knows how to aid others in gaining such a mastery as may be obtained by the study of a book."

The Field.—"We are not in the least surprised that a third edition of this useful and eminently practical book should be called for. On former occasions we were able to speak of it in terms of commendation, and this edition is worthy of equal praise."

Baily's Magazine.—"An eminently practical teacher, whose theories are the outcome of experience, learned not in the study, but on the road, in the hunting field, and on the racecourse."

Sporting Times.—"We heartily commend it to our readers."

Illustrated Sporting and Dramatic News.—"The book is one that no man who has ever sat in a saddle can fail to read with interest."

The Graphic.—"Is as practical as Captain Horace Hayes' 'Veterinary Notes' and 'Guide to Horse Management in India.' Greater praise than this it is impossible to give."

W. THACKER & CO., 87 NEWGATE STREET, LONDON.

THACKER, SPINK & CO., CALCUTTA.

Uniform with "Riding," etc. 21s.

ILLUSTRATED HORSE-BREAKING

BY

Capt. M. H. HAYES.

1. Theory of Breaking.
2. Principles of Mounting.
3. Horse Control.
4. Rendering Docile.
5. Giving Good Mouths.
6. Teaching to Jump.
7. Mounting for First Time.
8. Breaking for Ladies' Riding.
9. Breaking to Harness.
10. Faults of Mouth.
11. Nervousness and Impatience of Control.
12. Jibbing.
13. Jumping Faults.
14. Faults in Harness.
15. Aggressiveness.
16. Riding and Driving Newly-broken Horse.
17. Stable Vices.
18. Teaching Circus Tricks.

"The work is eminently practical and readable."—*Veterinary Journal.*

"Clearly explained in simple, practical language, made all the more clear by a set of capital drawings."—*Scotsman.*

"It is characteristic of all Captain Hayes' books on Horses that they are eminently practical, and the present one is no exception to the rule. A work which is entitled to high praise as being far and away the best reasoned-out book on Breaking under a new system we have seen."—*Field.*

WITH FIFTY-ONE ILLUSTRATIONS BY J. H. OSWALD BROWN.

W. THACKER & CO., 87 *NEWGATE STREET, LONDON.*

Foolscap 4to, 34s.

THE POINTS OF THE HORSE.
A familiar treatise on Equine Conformation.
By Capt. M. H. HAYES, F.R.C.V.S.

DESCRIBING THE POINTS IN WHICH THE
PERFECTION OF EACH CLASS
OF HORSES CONSISTS.

*Illustrated by 76 reproductions of Photographs of Typical Horses,
and 204 Drawings, chiefly by* J. H. OSWALD BROWN.

W. THACKER & CO., 87 NEWGATE STREET, LONDON.

THACKER, SPINK & CO., CALCUTTA.

THE POINTS OF THE HORSE.

Times. — "An elaborate and instructive compendium of sound knowledge on a subject of great moment to all owners of horses, by a writer of established authority on all matters connected with the horse."

Army and Navy Gazette. — "It is scientific in its method, and practical in its purpose."

Nature. — "A soldier, a certificated veterinarian, a traveller and a successful rider, the author is well qualified to treat on all that pertains to the subject before us."

The Referee. — "What Captain Hayes does not know about horses is probably not particularly worth knowing."

Saturday Review. — "This is another of Captain Hayes' good books on the horse, and to say it is the best would not be going far out of the way of truth. It is a luxurious book, well got up, well and clearly printed in large readable type, and profusely illustrated."

Pall Mall Budget. — "A volume that must be regarded as the standard work on the subject. It is well done. No point is left unexplained; no quality in a type unnoticed."

Sporting Times. — "The best production of its kind we have seen."

Field. — "To those who are desirous of availing themselves of the knowledge of a writer who has been used to horses all his life, the book may be cordially recommended."

Veterinary Journal. — "No book like this has hitherto appeared in English, or any other language. For giving us such a beautiful, interesting and instructive book, the members of the veterinary profession, horsemen and horse owners, as well as delineators of the horse, in every English speaking country, must acknowledge themselves deeply indebted to Captain Hayes."

THACKER, SPINK & CO., CALCUTTA.

In Imperial 16mo. Illustrated. 8s. 6d.

INDIAN RACING REMINISCENCES:
BEING
ENTERTAINING NARRATIVES AND ANECDOTES OF MEN, HORSES, AND SPORT.

Illustrated with Twenty-Two Portraits and a Number of Smaller Engravings.

By CAPTAIN M. HORACE HAYES.

"The book is full of racy anecdote, and the author writes so kindly of his brother office and the sporting planters with whom he came into contact, that one cannot help admiring the genial and happy temperament of the author."—*Bell's Life.*

"Captain Hayes shows himself a thorough master of his subject, and has so skilfully interwoven technicalities, history, and anecdote, that the last page comes all too soon."—*Field.*

·Fifth Edition. Revised. Crown 8vo. 9s.

TRAINING & HORSE MANAGEMENT IN INDIA.

By CAPTAIN M. HORACE HAYES, F.R.C.V.S.

"No better guide could be placed in the hands of either amateur horseman or veterinary surgeon."—*The Veterinary Journal.*

"A useful guide in regard to horses anywhere. Concise, practical, and portable."—*Saturday Review.*

W. THACKER & CO., 87 NEWGATE STREET, LONDON.

THACKER, SPINK & CO., CALCUTTA.

Crown 8vo. Uniform with "Veterinary Notes." 8s. 6d.

SOUNDNESS AND AGE OF HORSES.
WITH ONE HUNDRED AND SEVENTY ILLUSTRATIONS.

A Complete Guide to all those features which require attention when purchasing Horses, distinguishing mere defects from the symptoms of unsoundness; with explicit instructions how to conduct an examination of the various parts.

BY CAPTAIN M. H. HAYES, F.R.C.V.S.

"Captain Hayes is entitled to much credit for the explicit and sensible manner in which he has discussed the many questions—some of them extremely vexed ones—which pertain to soundness and unsoundness in horses."—*Veterinary Journal.*

"Captain Hayes' work is evidently the result of much careful research, and the horseman, as well as the veterinarian, will find in it much that is interesting and instructive."—*Field.*

W. THACKER & CO., 87 NEWGATE STREET, LONDON.

THACKER, SPINK & CO., CALCUTTA.

In Imperial 16mo. Uniform with "Lays of Ind," "Hindu Mythology," etc. *Handsomely bound.* 10s. 6d.

RIDING FOR LADIES.
With Hints on the Stable.
BY MRS. POWER O'DONOGHUE.
AUTHOR OF "LADIES ON HORSEBACK," "A BEGGAR ON HORSEBACK," ETC.

With 91 Illustrations drawn expressly for the Work by A. Chantrey Corbould.

THIS able and beautiful volume will form a Standard on the Subject, and is one which no lady can dispense with. The scope of the work will be understood by the following:

CONTENTS.
I. Ought Children to Ride?
II. "For Mothers & Children."
III. First Hints to a Learner.
IV. Selecting a Mount.
V., VI. The Lady's Dress.
VII. Bitting. VIII. Saddling.
IX. How to Sit, Canter, &c.
X. Reins, Voice, and Whip.
XI. Riding on the Road.
XII. Paces, Vices, and Faults.
XIII. A Lesson in Leaping.
XIV. Managing Refusers.
XV. Falling.
XVI. Hunting Outfit Considered.
XVII. Economy in Riding Dress.
XVIII. Hacks and Hunters.
XIX. In the Hunting Field.
XX. Shoeing. XXI. Feeding.
XXII. Stabling. XXIII. Doctoring.
XXIV. Breeding. XXV. "Tips."

"When there may arise differences of opinion as to some of the suggestions contained in this volume, the reader, especially if a woman, may feel assured she will not go far astray in accepting what is said by one of her own sex, who has the distinction of three times beating the Empress of Austria in the hunting field, from whom she 'took the brush.' 'Riding for Ladies' is certain to become a classic."
—*New York Sportsman.*

W. THACKER & CO., 87 NEWGATE STREET, LONDON.

THACKER, SPINK & CO., CALCUTTA.

Crown 8vo.   7s. 6d.
A TEA PLANTER'S LIFE IN ASSAM.
By GEORGE M. BARKER.
WITH 75 ILLUSTRATIONS.

This book aims at conveying to all interested in India and the tea industry an entertaining and useful account of the topographical features of Assam; the strange surroundings—human and animal—of the European resident; the trying climate; the daily life of the planter; and general details of the formation and working of tea gardens.

"Mr. Barker has supplied us with a very good and readable description, accompanied by numerous illustrations drawn by himself. What may be called the business parts of the book are of most value."—*Contemporary Review.*

"Cheery, well-written little book."—*Graphic.*

"A very interesting and amusing book, artistically illustrated from sketches drawn by the author."—*Mark Lane Express.*

LIST OF THE TEA GARDENS OF INDIA AND CEYLON.

Their Acreage, Managers, Assistants, Calcutta Agents, Coolie Depôts, Proprietors, Companies, Directors, Capital, London Agents and Factory Marks, by which any chest may be identified. Also embraces Coffee, Indigo, Silk, Sugar, Cinchona, Lac, Cardamom and other Concerns. 8vo. Sewed, 6s.

"The strong point of the book is the reproduction of the factory marks, which are presented side by side with the letterpress. To buyers of tea and other Indian products on this side, the work needs no recommendation."—*British Trade Journal.*

W. THACKER & CO., 87 NEWGATE STREET, LONDON.

Crown 8vo. 7s. 6d.

THE INDIGO MANUFACTURER.

A Practical and Theoretical Guide

FROM THE RECEIPT OF THE PLANT TO THE PRODUCTION OF THE CAKE

With numerous EXPERIMENTS illustrating the Scientific Principles bearing on each Phase of the Manufacture.

By J. BRIDGES-LEE, M.A., F.C.S., F.Z.S., F.R.A.S. Bengal, etc., etc.

"It enlightens us on a matter about which our knowledge till now has been highly barren and uncertain—the technicalities of the winning of the Indigo from its Indian home. Each operation which the Indigo has to undergo before its perfection has a separate chapter. At the end of each, experiments are described which are to serve this purpose, so that the object for which the pourtrayed operation is given is made clear and put in a right light."—*Chemiker Zeitung* (Translated).

In Crown 8vo. 7s. 6d.

THE CULTURE AND MANUFACTURE OF INDIGO:

WITH DESCRIPTION OF A PLANTER'S LIFE AND RESOURCES.

By W. M. REID.

WITH NINETEEN ILLUSTRATIONS BY THE AUTHOR.

"A concise and readable manual, not only of everything relating to the industry, but of the whole round of business and recreation that makes up the Planter's life. . . . The writer is at once accurate and graphic, and on the strength merely of reading these bright pages one almost feels competent to take full charge of a 'concern.'"—*Englishman.*

W. THACKER & CO., 87 NEWGATE STREET, LONDON.

THACKER, SPINK & CO., CALCUTTA.

Uniform with "Lays of Ind," "Riding," etc. 10s. 6d.

HINDU MYTHOLOGY:
VEDIC AND PURANIC.

BY

REV. W. J. WILKINS,

OF THE LONDON MISSIONARY
SOCIETY, CALCUTTA.

*Illustrated by One Hundred Engravings
chiefly from Drawings by Native Artists.*

REVIEWS.

"His aim has been to give a faithful account of the Hindu deities such as an intelligent native would himself give, and he has endeavoured, in order to achieve his purpose, to keep his mind free from prejudice or theological bias. To help to completeness he has included a number of drawings of the principal deities, executed by native artists. The author has attempted a work of no little ambition and has succeeded in his attempt, the volume being one of great interest and usefulness; and not the less so because he has strictly refrained from diluting his facts with comments of his own. It has numerous illustrations."—*Home News.*

"Mr. Wilkins has done his work well, with an honest desire to state facts apart from all theological prepossession, and his volume is likely to be a useful book of reference."—*Guardian.*

"In Mr. Wilkins' book we have an illustrated manual, the study of which will lay a solid foundation for more advanced knowledge, while it will furnish those who may have the desire without having the time or opportunity to go further into the subject, with a really extensive stock of accurate information."—*Indian Daily News.*

W. THACKER & CO., 87 NEWGATE STREET, LONDON.

THACKER, SPINK & CO., CALCUTTA.

H. E. BUSTEED'S "ECHOES FROM OLD CALCUTTA."

A MOST INTERESTING SERIES OF SKETCHES OF CALCUTTA LIFE, CHIEFLY TOWARDS THE CLOSE OF THE LAST CENTURY. Second Edition. Post 8vo. Rs. 6. (8s. 6d.) With Numerous Illustrations.

Door of Black Hole.   Grated Windows.

THE "BLACK HOLE" OF CALCUTTA.

"It is a pleasure to reiterate the warm commendation of this instructive and lively volume which its appearance called forth some few years since. It would be lamentable if a book so brought with interest to all Englishmen should be restricted to Anglo-Indian circles. A fresh instalment of letters from Warren Hastings to his wife must be noted as extremely interesting, while the papers on Sir Philip Francis, Nuncomar, and the romantic career of Mrs. Grand, who became Princess Benevento and the wife of Talleyrand, ought to now be widely known."—*Saturday Review.*

"Dr. Busteed has unearthed some astonishing revelations of what European Life in India resembled a century back."—*Daily Telegraph.*

W. THACKER & CO., 87 NEWGATE STREET, LONDON.

THACKER, SPINK & CO., CALCUTTA.

300 Illustrations. Imperial 16mo. 12s. 6d.
A HANDBOOK OF INDIAN FERNS.
By COLONEL R. H. BEDDOME, F.L.S.,
Late Conservator of Forests, Madras.

"It is the first special book of portable size and moderate price which has been devoted to Indian Ferns, and is in every way deserving of the extensive circulation it is sure to obtain."—*Nature.*

"I have just seen a new work on Indian Ferns which will prove vastly interesting, not only to the Indian people, but to the botanists of this country."—*Indian Daily News.*

"The 'Ferns of India.' This is a good book, being of a useful and trustworthy character. The species are familiarly described, and most of them illustrated by small figures."—*Gardeners' Chronicle.*

"Those interested in botany will do well to procure a new work on the 'Ferns of British India.' The work will prove a first-class text book."—*Free Press.*

3s. 6d.
SUPPLEMENT to the FERNS OF BRITISH INDIA, etc.
By COLONEL R. H. BEDDOME.

Containing Ferns which have been discovered since the publication of "The Handbook to the Ferns of British India," etc.

NEARLY READY.
HOW TO CHOOSE A DOG, & HOW TO SELECT A PUPPY.
TOGETHER WITH A FEW NOTES UPON THE PECULIARITIES AND CHARACTERISTICS OF EACH BREED.
By VERO SHAW,
Author of " The Illustrated Book of the Dog," late Kennel Editor of the " Field."

This small work will give in a brief, yet compendious form, the various Breeds—their Characteristics—Points—Average Weights at various Ages from six weeks to full growth—Points to look for in choosing average age at which the breed arrives at maturity, etc. The book is prepared in response to the innumerable inquiries showered upon the Author in his editorial capacity, and will form an invaluable guide in the selection of Dogs, as well as an aide-memoir to all.

W. THACKER & CO., 87 NEWGATE STREET, LONDON.

Crown 8vo. Illustrated. *Rs.* 5; Interleaved, *Rs.* 5-8.

A TEXT BOOK
OF
INDIAN BOTANY:
MORPHOLOGICAL,
PHYSIOLOGICAL,
and SYSTEMATIC.

By W. H. GREGG,
Lecturer on Botany, Hughli College.

With 240 Illustrations.

Crown 8vo. *7s. 6d.* Illustrated.

MANUAL OF
AGRICULTURE FOR INDIA.
By Lieut. F. POGSON.

1. Origin and Character of Soils.—2. Ploughing and Preparing for Seed.—3. Manures and Composts.—4. Wheat Cultivation.—5. Barley.—6. Oats.—7. Rye.—8. Rice.—9. Maize.—10. Sugar-producing Sorghums.—11. Common Sorghums.—12. Sugarcane.—13. Oil Seed.—14. Field Pea Crops.—15. Dall or Pulse.—16. Root Crops.—17. Cold Spice.—18. Fodder.—19. Water-Nut.—20. Ground-Nut.—21. Rush-Nut or Chufas.—22. Cotton.—23. Tobacco.—24. Mensuration.—Appendix.

"A work of extreme practical value."—*Home News.*

"Mr. Pogson's advice may be profitably followed by both native and European agriculturists, for it is eminently practical and devoid of empiricism. His little volume embodies the teaching of a large and varied experience, and deserves to be warmly supported."—*Madras Mail.*

W. THACKER & CO., 87 *NEWGATE STREET, LONDON.*

THACKER, SPINK & CO., CALCUTTA.

Fourth Edition, Imperial 16mo. 15r. Illustrated.

A MANUAL OF GARDENING
FOR
BENGAL AND UPPER INDIA.

By THOMAS A. C. FIRMINGER, M.A.

THOROUGHLY REVISED AND BROUGHT DOWN TO THE PRESENT TIME BY

J. H. JACKSON,
Editor of " The Indian Agriculturist."

PART I.
OPERATIONS OF GARDENING.
Chap. I.—Climate—Soils—Manures.
Chap. II.—Laying-out a Garden—Lawns —Hedges—Hoeing and Digging—Drainage — Conservatories — Betel Houses—Decorations—Implements—Shades—Labels—Vermin—Weeds.
Chap. III.—Seeds—Seed Sowing—Pot Culture—Planting—Cuttings—Layers —Gootee—Grafting and Inarching—Budding—Pruning and Root Pruning —Conveyance.
Chap. IV. Calendar of Operations.

PART II.
GARDEN PLANTS.
1. Culinary Vegetables.
2. Dessert Fruits.
3. Edible Nuts.
4. Ornamental Annuals.
5. Ornamental Trees, Shrubs, and Herbaceous Perennials.

Crown 8vo, cloth. *Rs.* 2-8.

THE AMATEUR GARDENER IN THE HILLS.
HINTS FROM VARIOUS AUTHORITIES ON GARDEN MANAGEMENT,
AND ADAPTED TO THE HILLS;
WITH HINTS ON FOWLS, PIGEONS, AND RABBIT KEEPING;
And various Recipes connected with the above subjects which are not commonly found in Recipe Books.

W. THACKER & CO., 87 NEWGATE STREET, LONDON.

THACKER, SPINK & CO., CALCUTTA.

Thacker's Guide Books.

Agra and its Neighbourhood: A Handbook for Visitors. By H. G. KEENE, C.S. Fifth Edition, Revised. Maps, Plans, &c. Fcap. 8vo, cloth. Rs. 2-8.

Allahabad, Cawnpore and Lucknow. By H. G. KEENE, C.S. Second Edition, Re-written and Enlarged. Fcap. 8vo.

Burma and its People, Manners, Customs and Religion. By Capt. C. J. V. S. FORBES. 8vo. Rs. 4 (7s. 6d.).

Burmah Myam-Ma: the Home of the Burman. By TSAYA (Rev. H. POWELL). Crown 8vo. Rs. 2 (3s. 6d.).

Calcutta, Thacker's Guide to. With Chapters on its Bypaths, &c., and a Chapter on the Government of India. Fcap. 8vo. With Maps. Rs. 2.

Calcutta to Liverpool by China, Japan and America, in 1877. By Lieut.-General Sir HENRY NORMAN. Second Edition. Fcap. 8vo, cloth. Rs. 2-8 (3s. 6d.).

Darjeeling and its Neighbourhood. By S. MITCHELL, M.A. With two Maps. Rs. 2.

Delhi and its Neighbourhood, A Handbook for Visitors to. By H. G. KEENE, C.S. Third Edition. Maps. Fcap. 8vo, cloth. Rs. 2-8.

India, Thacker's Map, in case, 8s. 6d.

India, Map of the Civil Divisions of; including Governments, Divisions and Districts, Political Agencies and Native States; also the Cities and Towns. Re. 1.

Kashmir Handbook (Ince's). Revised and Re-written. By Surg.-Major JOSHUA DUKE. With 4 Maps. Fcap. 8vo, cloth. Rs. 6-8.

Kashgaria (Eastern or Chinese Turkestan), Historical, Geographical, Military and Industrial. By Col. KUROPATKIN, Russian Army. Translated by Major GOWAN, H. M.'s Indian Army. 8vo. Rs. 6-8.

Kumaun Lakes, Angling in the. With a Map of the Kumaun Lake Country. By Depy. Surg.-Genl. W. WALKER. Crown 8vo, cloth. Rs. 4. "Written with all the tenderness and attention to detail which characterise the followers of the gentle art."—*Hayes' Sporting News.*

Lucknow, Tourists' Guide to. Plans. Rs. 2.

Masuri, Landaur, Dehra Dun, and the Hills North of Dehra; including Routes to the Snows and other places of note; with chapter on Garhwal (Tehri), Hardwar, Rurki, and Chakrata. By JOHN NORTHAM. Rs. 2-8.

Simla, The Hills Beyond. Three Months' Tour from Simla ("In the Footsteps of the Few") through Bussahir, Kunowar, and Spiti, to Lahoul. By Mrs. J. C. MURRAY-AYNSLEY. Crown 8vo, cloth. Rs. 3.

Gold, Copper and Lead in Chota Nagpore. Compiled by Dr. W. KING, Director Geological Survey of India, and T. A. POPE, Dep. Supt. Survey of India. With Map of Geological Formation and the Areas taken up by the various Prospecting and Mining Companies. Crown 8vo, cloth. Rs. 5.

Russian Conversation-Grammar (on the System of Otto). With Exercises, Colloquial Phrases, and an English-Russian Vocabulary. By A. KINLOCH, late Interpreter to H.B.M. Consulate, St. Petersburg. 9s. On the system of Otto, with Illustrations, phrases and idioms; leading by easy and rapid gradations to a colloquial knowledge of the Language.

W. THACKER & CO., 87 *NEWGATE STREET, LONDON.*

The Reconnoitrer's Guide and Field Book, adapted for India. By Major M. J. KING-HARMAN, B.S.C. Third Edition, Revised and in great part re-written. In roan. *Rs.* 4.
Can be used as an ordinary Pocket Note Book, or as a Field Message Book; the pages are ruled as a Field Book, and in sections, for written description or sketch. "To officers serving in India this guide will be invaluable."—*Broad Arrow.*

Tales from Indian History: being the Annals of India retold in Narratives. By J. TALBOYS WHEELER. Sixth Edition. Crown 8vo, cloth gilt. 3s. 6d.

Hindustani as it ought to be Spoken. A Manual with Explanations, Vocabularies and Exercises. By J. TWEEDIE, C.S. Second Edition. *Rs.* 2-8.

A Memoir of the late Justice Onoocool Chunder Mookerjee. By M. MOOKERJEE. Third Edition. 12mo. *Re.* 1.
"A most interesting and amusing illustration of Indian English.
"The reader is earnestly advised to procure the life of this gentleman, written by his nephew, and read it."—*The Tribes on my Frontier.*

The Indian Cookery Book. A Practical Handbook to the Kitchen in India: adapted to the Three Presidencies. By a Thirty-five Years' Resident. *Rs.* 3.

Indian Notes about Dogs: their Diseases and Treatment. By Major C——. Third Edition, Revised. Fcap. 8vo, cloth. *Rs.* 1-8.

Indian Horse Notes: an Epitome of Useful Information. By Major C——, Author of "Indian Notes about Dogs." Second Edition, Enlarged. Fcap. 8vo, cloth. *Rs.* 2.

Horse-Breeding and Rearing in India: with Notes on Training for the Flat and Across Country; and on Purchase, Breaking-in, and General Management. By Major J. HUMFREY. Crown 8vo. *Rs.* 3-8.

Hygiene of Water and Water Supplies. By PATRICK HEHIR, M.D., F.R.C.S. Edin.; Lecturer on Hygiene, Hyderabad. Surgeon, Bengal Army. 8vo, limp cloth. *Rs.* 2.

Plain Tales from the Hills: A Collection of Stories by RUDYARD KIPLING. Third Edition. Crown 8vo. *Rs.* 4.
"They sparkle with fun; they are full of life, merriment and humour.'—*Allen's Indian Mail.*

A Text Book of Medical Jurisprudence for India. By I. B. LYON, C.I.E., F.G.S., F.I.C. Professor of Chemistry and Medical Jurisprudence Grant, Medical College, Bombay. Revised, as to the Legal Matter, by J. D. INVERARITY, Advocate of the High Court, Bombay. Medium 8vo. Illustrated. 25s.

The Management and Medical Treatment of Children in India. By EDWARD A. BIRCH, M.D., Surg.-Major, Bengal Establishment. Second Edition Revised (Being the Eighth Edition of "Goodeve's Hints"). Crown 8vo. 10s. 6d.

Our Administration of India. Being a Complete Account of the Revenue and Collectorate Administration in all Departments, with special reference to the Work and Duties of a District Officer in Bengal. By H. A. D. PHILLIPS. 6s.

The Indian Medical Service. A Guide for intended Candidates and for the Junior Officers of the Service. By W. W. WEBB, M.B., Bengal Army. Crown 8vo. *Rs.* 4.

Thacker's Indian Directory. Embracing the whole Territories under the Viceroy, with the Native States. Published Annually. 36s.

THACKER, SPINK & CO., CALCUTTA.

INDEX.

		Page
"Amateur Gardener in the Hills."	Rs. 2-8	37
Barker. "Tea Planter in Assam."	7/6	31
Beddome. "Ferns of India."	22/6	35
Birch. "Children in India."	10/6	39
Bridges-Lees. "Indigo Manufacturer."	7/6	32
Busteed. "Echoes from Old Calcutta."	8/6	34
Coldstream. "Grasses of the Punjab."	25/-	20
Eha. "Behind the Bungalow."	6/-	8
,, "Tribes on my Frontier."	8/6	6
,, "A Naturalist on the Prowl."		4
Firminger. "Gardening for India." By Jackson.	15/-	37
Forsyth. "Highlands of Central India."	7-8	20
Gracey. "Rhyming Legends of Ind."	6/-	11
Gregg. "Indian Botany."	5	36
Guide Books.		38
Hayes. "Veterinary Notes." 12/6	10/6	21-24
,, "Horsewoman." 10/6 "Illustrated Horse-Breaking."	21/-	22-25
,, "Points of the Horse." 34/- "Soundness and Age."	8/6	26-29
,, "Indian Racing." 8/6 "Training and Management."	9/-	28
Hehir. "Hygiene of Water."	2	39
Humfrey. "Horse-Breeding."		39
"Indian Cookery."	4/6	39
"Indian Notes—Dogs."	1-8	39
"Indian ,, Horses."	2	39
King and Pope. "Gold, Copper, Lead," &c.	5	38
King-Harman. "Reconnoitring."	4	39
Kinloch. "Large Game."	42/-	19
,, "Russian Grammar."	9/-	38
Kipling. "Plain Tales."	4	39
,, "Departmental Ditties."	5/-	11
"Lays of Ind." By Aliph Cheem.	10/6	10
Le Mesurier. "Game Birds."	15/-	28
Lyon. "Medical Jurisprudence."	25/-	39
Newland. "Image of War."		2
O'Donoghue. "Riding for Ladies."	10/6	39
"Onoocool Mookerjee, Life of."	1	39
Phillips. "Our Administration of India."	6/-	39
Pogson. "Agriculture for India."	7/6	36
Reid. "Indigo Planter."	7/6	32
Shaw. "Dogs for Hot Climates."		13
,, "How to Choose a Dog," etc.		35
Sterndale. "Denizens of the Jungle."	16/-	17
,, "Mammalia of India."	22/6	16
,, "Seonee."	8/6	15
"Tea Gardens of India and Ceylon."	6/6	31
Thacker's Guide Books, various.		38
,, "Indian Directory."	36/-	39
,, "Map of India."	8/6	38
Tweedie. "How to Speak Hindustani."	2-8	39
Tweed. "Cow Keeping in India."	6/-	12
,, "Poultry Keeping in India."		14
Tyacke. "Sportsman's Manual," &c.	3-8	17
Webb. "Indian Medical Service."	5/6	39
Wheeler. "Tales from Indian History."	3/6	39
Wilkins. "Hindu Mythology."	10/6	33

W. THACKER & CO., 87 NEWGATE STREET, LONDON.

www.ingramcontent.com/pod-product-compliance
Lightning Source LLC
Chambersburg PA
CBHW032059230426
43662CB00035B/747